The Commissions
   are Bigger!
The Bonuses are
   Higher!
A Guide to Selling
BIG-TICKET GOODS
   AND SERVICES

The Commissions are Bigger! The Bonuses are Higher! A Guide to Selling BIG-TICKET GOODS AND SERVICES

MILTON M. HARRIS

DOW JONES-IRWIN
Homewood, Illinois 60430

© DOW JONES-IRWIN, 1981

All rights reserved. No part of this publication may be reproduced, stored in a retrieval system, or transmitted, in any form or by any means, electronic, mechanical, photocopying, recording, or otherwise, without the prior written permission of the publisher.

This publication is designed to provide accurate and authoritative information in regard to the subject matter covered. It is sold with the understanding that the publisher is not engaged in rendering legal, accounting, or other professional service. If legal advice or other expert assistance is required, the services of a competent professional person should be sought.

From a Declaration of Principles jointly adopted by a Committee of the American Bar Association and a Committee of Publishers.

ISBN 0-87094-263-8
Library of Congress Catalog Card No. 80–70924
Printed in the United States of America

1 2 3 4 5 6 7 8 9 0 K 8 7 6 5 4 3 2 1

Preface

The purpose of this book is to assist you in becoming successful in big-ticket financial sales. For some this book may serve as a primer—a means for helping you establish yourself in a sales career. For most, however, this volume should be used as a guide to reevaluating and reorganizing your sales career.

For 25 years I have made my living in financial sales, first as a stockbroker and later as a sales executive for leasing services. In all this time, I have been selling and training others to sell. And always I come to the same conclusion: Financial sales are both fascinating and demanding. They provide plenty of opportunities for the salesman to demonstrate his initiative and daring, but success depends on determination and a solid knowledge of the basics.

It is certainly true that a good salesman must have many positive characteristics. In my opinion, being a problem solver is the most valuable service you can provide for a client. Understanding a customer's needs and answering those needs with a solid financial package is what salesmanship is all about.

Milton M. Harris

Contents

1. **The making of a big-ticket financial salesman, 1**

   Characteristics of successful salesmen. The power of persistence. Problem-solving and communication skills. Successful salesmen at work: *Persistence always pays. People get what they pay for. Mutual trust pays off. Don't take no for an answer.*

2. **Projecting the image of success, 17**

   How to get your story across: *Analysis of speaking ability. Speaking techniques.* How to look the part: *Dressing according to plan. Ways to economize. Tips on traveling. A final suggestion.*

3. **Selling is a state of mind, 31**

   The nature of selling. First things first. From loser to winner. Playing the game to win.

4. **What to do before the first interview, 39**

   Building a knowledge base: *What to look for in* The Wall Street Journal. *Other general information sources.* Gathering information on prospects and competitors. Preparing to proceed.

5. **Prospecting, 47**

   Finding the hidden treasure. Prospecting for individual sales: *Step 1. Step 2. Step 3. Step 4. Step 5. Step 6. Sources of individual prospects. Cold calls can find hot prospects.* Prospecting for corporate sales: *Step 1. Step 2. Step 3. Step 4. Step 5. Step 6.* The mechanics of prospecting.

6. **The interview, 69**

   Interviewing basics: *Getting paid for a blind date.* Problems encountered in interviews: *Welcoming objections. Uncovering hidden objections. Converting to dollars and cents. Finding the decision maker.*

7. Issuing proposals, 81

   Legal complexities: *The law of contracts. Laws concerning fraud.* Procedures and safeguards.

8. Follow-up, 101

   Types of follow-up. Tools of the trade.

9. Negotiating, 107

   Rules for negotiating.

10. Closing, 113

    Examples of closings: Faint heart never wins.

11. Getting home office support, 121

12. A note to the saleswoman, 125

Summary: Selling can be fun, or winning beats losing, 129

1 | The making of a big-ticket financial salesman

Anyone in the field of big-ticket financial sales or who anticipates entering it can expect to earn at least $3 million over his working life. This includes stockbrokers, mutual fund salesmen, equipment leasing salesmen, lending officers for banks or finance companies, life insurance salesmen, tax shelter advisors, and salesmen for a hundred varied financial services. It includes women as well as men; though there are very few women in big-ticket sales, the field certainly is open to them. The potential monetary value of such careers is enormous, but everyone who aspires to be a big-ticket financial salesperson will not succeed.

This chapter points out the characteristics of successful financial salesmen and demonstrates how these characteristics affect the way they work in actual situations. If you honestly evaluate your own character and personality in relation to the characteristics identified and demonstrated in these examples, you should be able to estimate your own possibilities of success in this demanding field. The checklist of potential for salesmen of financial services which is given in this chapter is an aid in doing this.

CHECKLIST FOR RATING YOUR POTENTIAL AS A SALESMAN OF FINANCIAL SERVICES

You can rate your potential as a prospective salesman of financial services with the following checklist. Rate yourself honestly on each question and then determine what you think of your prospects.

The questions should be rated as follows:
- 4—definitely yes
- 3—maybe
- 2—definitely no
- 1—don't know

The higher the score, the greater the potential.

1. Am I as comfortable working alone as I am in a group situation?
2. Am I comfortable convincing people to do things they don't want to do?
3. Do I finish what I start, regardless of obstacles?
4. Do I welcome challenges?
5. Is the opportunity to earn "big money" more important than a steady salary?
6. Do I easily understand people and their motivation?
7. Do I read *The Wall Street Journal* daily?
8. Do I enjoy reading financial or business publications?
9. Can I mentally add and subtract numbers and do simple division and multiplication?
10. Do I hate to lose?
11. Am I self-confident?
12. Do I make my own decisions without consulting anyone?
13. Am I generally cheerful and optimistic even when surrounded by problems?
14. Do I have the willpower to force myself to do things that hurt in order to reach my goals?
15. Do people generally react favorably to me?
16. Do I easily put myself in another's place, thus understanding why he reacts as he does?
17. Can I say "no" and stick to it despite pressure?

18. Am I in good health?
19. Do I do what I think is right regardless of the opinions of others?
20. Can I fail 100 times and try again?
21. In conversation, do I easily express my ideas?
22. Do I analyze problems well?
23. Can I describe myself in three short paragraphs?
24. Am I patient when I must be?

The general conception of a successful salesperson is one who has a pleasing appearance, the ability to speak easily, a sharp mind, and a generally positive attitude. But some people with these characteristics fail as salespersons, while others who have an unimpressive appearance and halting speech habits and who seem to be unable to impress anyone are remarkably successful. The reason for these apparently inconsistent results is that the impression the salesperson makes on others is determined by evidence of fundamental personal characteristics which have stronger, more lasting effects than outward appearances do.

CHARACTERISTICS OF SUCCESSFUL SALESMEN

In my experience, successful salesmen generally have the following characteristics:

1. Intelligence—defined as the ability to understand and solve problems.
2. Empathy—defined as an imaginative projection of one's own being into another's, such as the ability to identify with what another person is thinking and understand why.
3. Sympathy—defined as reciprocal liking and understanding.
4. Ego strength—defined as the ability to hear "nos" and try to turn them into "yesses," and a total determination to succeed.

Of these four qualities, the ability to take no for an answer and not become discouraged is the most important. In almost every way, a child is conditioned from birth to get along by going along. This may mean different things in different cultures, but almost universally it means that if you want to be liked, you must learn to fit into a pattern. You must not be overly aggressive; you must not force others to do things they do not want to do.

After 20-some years of such conditioning, it is no wonder that the average individual who tries to become a salesman finds it necessary to make a complete 360-degree turn from everything he has been taught by his family, school, and peers. Make no mistake, a good salesman, meaning a successful salesman, must have the ability to go against everything society usually considers acceptable behavior. This is the prime reason why clean-cut, hard-working, positive-thinking young people fail by the thousands as salespersons. They may have the exemplary characteristics, but these are not sufficient to ensure success in selling if they cannot endure rejection many times each day.

This fear of rejection is one reason that very few average high school or college graduates voluntarily choose careers as salespersons. Their perceptions of salespersons fit an inaccurate stereotype. They view the successful salesman as a cigar-smoking, joking, heavy-drinking, fun-loving extrovert who most likely would sell a defective car to his aging grandmother. The perceived combination of unpleasant personal characteristics and low ethical standards tends to "turn off" any youths who might have been thinking along these lines.

I don't know if this stereotype *ever* represented the successful salesman. I can assure you, however, that it doesn't now represent a successful salesman of big-ticket financial sales. The most successful security salesman I have ever known began as a salesman for a major securities firm. He neither drinks nor smokes, and he never jokes. He is at his desk from 8:30 A.M. until 5:00 P.M. every day and rarely goes out for lunch. His free time is spent studying the market. He never lies or alibis when his recommendations result in losses for his clients, and he never brags when his recommendations are successful. He dresses neatly and conservatively. I believe he has earned well over $100,000 a year for at least the past ten years. If you met him, you might guess that he was an office worker of some type. You certainly wouldn't think he was a successful salesman.

The most successful life insurance salesman I know has very

much the same characteristics, but much of his work day, as well as his evenings and weekends, is spent making contacts. While he spends a substantial amount of time in his office, most of his work is done outside it, averaging 40 to 60 hours a week. He doesn't smoke, drinks little, and is generally quiet and reserved in his speech. He looks more like a high school football coach than a successful salesman, since he generally dresses in a sports coat and slacks. But he was one of the first life insurance salesmen in Baltimore to obtain his CLU. He has consistently stayed ahead of his peers in the market as far as dedication and competence are concerned.

Most of the successful salesmen in equipment leasing, mutual funds, insurance, securities, and other financial services I have known over the years have been cut from very much the same cloth as these two individuals. They may differ in some exterior features, but they generally are hard working, temperate, and intelligent. They all are far from the successful salesman stereotype which prevails in the minds of many people today.

Personality and charisma are often cited as characteristics successful salespersons should have. This has not been my experience. I have found that a simple, direct approach is the most effective way to sell financial products. The problem is not how to turn on the prospect but how to keep from turning *off* the prospect. An unusual appearance or manner is more apt to be offensive than effective. An involved or obviously phony approach can be disastrous. This is not a business where mere charm leads to success, since long negotiations are the rule rather than the exception. A person must be able to wear well over a period of time. Inspiring trust is more important than inspiring liking or even friendship.

THE POWER OF PERSISTENCE

An essential part of the psychological make-up of a successful salesman of financial services is determination. This is more important than any other character trait. Ray Kroc, the founder of McDonald's restaurants, has said: "Nothing in the world can take the place of persistence. Talent will not; nothing is more common than unsuccessful men with talent. Genius will not;

unrewarded genius is almost a proverb. Education alone will not; the world is full of educated derelicts. Persistence and determination alone are omnipotent."

Because the salesman of financial services must seek out prospects, and the ratio of sales to prospects is extremely low, a persistent desire to succeed is the most important characteristic he can have. Sometimes this determination is fueled by greed, or the desire for financial success, sometimes by fear of failure, and sometimes by ego, or the need to enhance self-esteem. In most men, it is a combination of these three factors that motivates their quest for success. Since in our society we keep score on success in terms of dollars, achieving financial rewards is not only a sign of success, it also provides a means to acquire material goods and thus gain status among peers, which improves our self-esteem. This is the way we win in the game of life, so we will push ourselves past fatigue, past discouragement, and past the loss of many of life's amenities in order to achieve financial success.

In my own case, a handicapped daughter and the need to provide for her future changed me from a 35-year-old cipher into a determined salesman. I was promoted to vice president of a major leasing company in three years and to the post of president of another company six years later. During that time, my total compensation increased almost 1,000 percent. It was determination that had been lacking, and acquiring it made a significant difference.

PROBLEM-SOLVING AND COMMUNICATION SKILLS

The most important asset a salesman of financial services can offer clients is his skills as a problem solver. The successful salesman is able to become a problem solver for clients because he understands others and can put himself in their place. He is empathetic as well as intelligent; he can understand his prospective client's problems and how the client views them. He sees the entire picture, from both sides.

Professional financial services salesmen are analysts who can draw inferences about the particular from references to the general. Most are familiar with the theoretical and practical aspects of interest fluctuation as they affect corporate financing and the bond market. They understand the stock market, investment alternatives, tax shelters, life and casualty insurance of various types, and general business conditions in the United States and around the world. In short, they have at least an acquaintance with most happenings in the business world.

An earnest young person who is graduated from college with a C average probably will not succeed in financial sales if the grades are indicative of his intelligence. Through the years, against my better judgment, I have hired clean-cut, earnest young persons who appeared to have all the requirements for success and then reluctantly, as it became evident that they didn't have the brainpower to succeed, let them go. Although they looked impressive, they lacked a general knowledge of business and the ability to find the information and apply it in solving specific problems.

Today's professional financial salesman must have an above-average ability to communicate ideas in person, over the telephone, and in written form. He needs to be able to share ideas with both prospective clients and co-workers. Clear, concise communications which quickly "get to the bottom line," are essential.

The most effective way to solve problems or to communicate is with the help of a mental outline in which the following questions are considered:

1. What is the problem to solved or discussed?
2. What are all the factors bearing upon the problem?
3. What is my recommendation?
4. Where do we go from here?

Simple, isn't it? Yet, many college graduates today lack the ability to think in this way. They seem to put any task in this order:

1. What do I want?
2. Can I get help or pass the task on to others?
3. If I can't pass the buck, can I do something else, preferably something that is easier?

A lesson in problem solving can be learned from an experience I had some years ago while I was selling securities. One day, after the market closed, an elderly gentleman stopped by my desk and asked if he might chat with me about his portfolio. He said that he had recently had a portfolio analysis done by a major brokerage firm and that he was unhappy with it. I took his list, which was considerable, and forwarded it to my firm's portfolio analysis group. In the meanwhile, I took the time to probe extensively into his objectives and his attachments to particular securities, if any.

About two weeks later the portfolio analysis from my firm came back and I presented it to him. He was no more satisfied than he had been previously, and I agreed with him. Both portfolio analysis groups, despite being told in very simple terms what his objectives were, had completely missed what he was attempting to accomplish. I therefore volunteered to do an analysis myself. Working at home for several evenings, I developed my idea of how to meet his objectives. When we again met, he was greatly pleased. He revealed that I had seen but a fraction of his holdings, which I eventually determined were well over $1 million in stocks. He had been testing me and my diligence before he revealed his true situation. After his portfolio was rearranged he introduced me to his sister-in-law, who had a substantial amount of securities, and several other relatives with major stock holdings.

Here was the type of customer any stockbroker would welcome. He had a large portfolio, and his objectives were very conservative and reasonable. He *wanted* to bring me additional business. In short, he was an ideal client. How did the many other brokers with whom he must have come in contact with let him get away? As I got to know him better, I realized that he was annoyed at being taken for granted. He was looking for individual service, and that was why I, a stranger, received his business although many of his acquaintances were stockbrokers.

SUCCESSFUL SALESMEN AT WORK

The examples of sales situations given in this section demonstrate the qualities required of today's professional financial salesman and illustrate how personal characteristics affect success. Each one also suggests lessons to be learned in the art of salesmanship.

Persistence always pays

Some years ago, a company leasing computers on a short-term basis required an inspection of the prospective lessee's installation by computer experts prior to writing a standard two-year lease. The purpose of the inspection was to determine how long the equipment would actually be used by the prospect, since the leasing company hoped to keep it in place considerably longer than the basic lease term. One of their salesmen had arranged the lease of a large-scale IBM computer to a major textile company. The salesman arrived at the prospect's office on Monday, met with the financial officer handling the transaction, introduced his firm's computer expert to the prospective lessee's manager of information services, and negotiated documents most of that day. Tuesday the salesman visited a nearby city to pursue other objectives. Later in the day he learned that the computer expert had refused to approve the transaction because, in his opinion, the computer lessee would be terminating promptly after two years, and the period of actual use would be too short for approval.

Although it was late in the day, well after 5:00 P.M., the salesman was successful in reaching his client and set up an appointment for 8:00 A.M. Wednesday. This meant he had to cancel his other appointments and travel a considerable distance, but he was there promptly the following morning. The financial officer was furious when he heard of the problem, since the computer was to be delivered that Friday morning, and it would be almost impossible to arrange alternative lease financing because of the loss of tax benefits once the equipment was installed.

The salesman, in an effort to prevent the transaction from being lost, pressed the client, and later the data processing manager, for facts which would enable him to dispute his own computer expert. His efforts kept him there through lunch and past dinner time, when the prospective lessees excused themselves. By Wednesday night the salesman had spent approximately 20 hours with the prospects and appeared about to lose the transaction. Thursday morning he was there again at 8:00 A.M., having canceled other appointments. By insistent questioning, he found that the computer expert's superior had had an unhappy experience with the prospective lessee some years before. Could it be that this superior was killing the transaction because of spite against the client? The client, with encouragement from the salesman, came to believe so.

Now the wrath of the lessee was directed at this individual rather than the leasing company. The salesman played on his client's irritation at the expert's superior and suggested that he would move heaven and earth to keep him from satisfying his revenge. The lessee's attitude completely changed, and it agreed to give additional warranties to the leasing company. Friday morning at 8:00, the fourth day of negotiations, the client met with the salesman and made arrangements to wire funds. The transaction was finally completed at 5:30 P.M. that day. The salesman had spent more than 48 hours with the client in order to salvage a major transaction.

The first lesson to be learned from this example is that a transaction is never won or lost until the final pieces of the agreement have been put together. In this case, persistence was necessary to avoid losing the sale. The second lesson is that you cannot solve a problem until you know precisely what the problem is, in all its dimensions. At first, this situation appeared to be a rather simple one: The lessee was going to use the equipment for a relatively short time, and there was no way to satisfy the lessor that it would be kept long enough to make the lease economically sound. The possible personal animosity of the data processing expert's boss may or may not have been significant, but in the mind of the lessee it was made to seem all-important. Once the lessee understood that the leasing company was not being arbitrary and wished to proceed with the transaction if at all possible, their anger was directed toward the computer expert and they began to cooperate with the salesman.

Another salesman visited a major utility for something like 15 years before he made his first sale. He did not make the mistake of spending a great deal of time with a company that was not an immediate prospect, but in a yearly telephone conversation he attempted to acquaint himself with as many aspects of the company's activities as possible and to supply such information as the prospect might find useful. When a situation arose where his product was needed, his persistence and helpfulness over the years paid off. The prospect felt that the business was almost owed to this salesman.

There are several lessons to be learned here. While a salesperson cannot reasonably expect to spend a great deal of time with a company that doesn't appear to be a prospect within the following 12 months at most, a certain amount of time must be spent on long-term prospects. Often, as in this case, an annual telephone call is sufficient. An honest, straightforward approach, coupled with knowledge of the product, will build up a considerable amount of confidence in the mind of a prospect over the years. Often salespersons are so intent on today's business that they fail to lay the necessary groundwork for future business. If you sincerely believe that you have a prospect, the time needed for an occasional telephone call will be well spent.

People get what they pay for

Another sales situation illustrating the necessity for the salesperson to determine what the prospect really wants is illustrated by the following experience of a salesman in the Midwest. The salesman was contacted by a major corporation and asked to develop a method of financing a subsidiary's product for its customers. The corporation had already contacted its bank, one of the nation's largest, to provide them with such a method, and it had called the salesman primarily as a courtesy, because of his prior contacts rather than out of any belief that his institution, which was much smaller, could provide a competitive method. The salesman obtained all the details, developed a complex proposal, and had it in the mail the next day. Within a week, he was visiting the prospect. The financial officer of the corporation said that its bank representative had indicated they would complete the transaction at a rate substantially lower than the one the salesman's institution was able to provide. The salesman then made the claim that his rate was actually lower than the competition's. When the stunned financial officer questioned this, since the numbers obviously indicated the contrary, the salesman repeated that his *rate* was lower, and the extra increment was not due to the rate but represented a charge for services rendered.

The salesman then asked a series of pointed questions. How long did it take the major bank to respond with a proposal? The answer was six weeks. How long had it taken him to respond? The answer was three days. How long did it take for the major bank to have a representative visit them? The answer was that no one had yet arrived. How long had it taken him to get there? The answer was one week. Did the major bank outline the specifics as to how this complex situation could be solved? The answer was no. Had the salesman's company indicated such an answer? The answer was yes. Thereupon the salesman said he would rest his case: "If, before the deal is completed, it takes six weeks for a proposal and you have not seen anybody, how often do you think you are going to see them after they have won your business?" After a few moments of silence, the financial officer agreed and the salesman won the deal.

The lesson to be learned from this situation is that one of the biggest mistakes a salesperson makes is to be defensive about the cost of the product being offered. Prospects don't really want products, they want some sort of result. The important thing is to obtain results for the prospect in a timely fashion. Cost is often secondary. If you can provide what a prospect *really* wants in a timely fashion, it is well worth the premium charged. I find very few prospects for any services who purchase anything for their own or their company's use on the basis of price alone. Almost invariably, quality has a significant effect on what they purchase. The problem is to convince them that quality in a financial service is just as important as quality in more tangible items.

If you are selling life insurance and your company's ten-year record of dividend payments is slightly under another company's, for example, this should really be insignificant to a prospective buyer. The past is not a guaranty of the future, and the important thing to a buyer of life insurance should be an adequately structured program of protection for loved ones. If you are selling securities and your competitor's commission schedule is lower than yours, this can be more than offset by the speed and accuracy with which you execute orders and provide timely, accurate information. If you are selling financial services of any other sort, such as mutual funds or tax shelters, and your competitor has a lower cost, you should stress your ability to structure your product in accordance with your prospect's needs and your readiness to cooperate and give support during the many unforeseen occurrences in a relationship.

The difficulty concerning price competition is usually more in the mind of the salesperson than in the mind of the prospect. A salesman of financial services must realize that expertise, integrity, flexibility, and the ability to satisfy the buyer's real needs are well worth almost any extra charge.

Mutual trust pays off

When an equipment leasing salesman made a "cold" telephone call on a large company, he was finally referred to an assistant treasurer whose task was to coordinate procurement of data processing equipment. The salesman first found the assistant treasurer to be unusually gruff and abrupt, and, feeling he had nothing to lose, asked if he or his company had unknowingly affronted the executive or the firm. The assistant treasurer's response was that he had negotiated a sale and leaseback contract for a substantial amount of data processing equipment with another leasing company which required the company to purchase the equipment as a preparatory step. At the last minute, because of lack of funds this leasing company had been forced to renege on the transaction. This caused the assistant treasurer a great deal of embarrassment with management, since the purchase was irrevocable and in effect the firm had bought a great deal of equipment it didn't want to own.

The salesman reassured the assistant treasurer as to his credentials and the credentials of his company. Although he did not receive much encouragement, he mad an appointment to see the executive the following week. At this meeting the assistant treasurer continued to be distant in manner, but he did supply enough information on his company's future computer plans to allow the salesman to issue a proposal. This proposal was hand delivered the following week, and since the savings were quite substantial, the salesman was able to point out some very positive benefits for the company. The assistant treasurer continued his negative attitude but also continued to supply information concerning the transaction.

At this point the salesman used what is known in the life insurance business as the "assumptive close"—he *assumed* that the company was going to proceed with the transaction. He instructed the assistant treasurer on how it could be easily consummated and "walked him through" the transaction. He closed the deal a few weeks later without ever having received any official final approval for it. The assistant treasurer never said explicitly, "I want to go ahead with this deal." The salesman went to great pains to assist the client in every step of the transaction so his fear of another disaster was effectively calmed. Subsequently the salesman leased another $15 million of equipment to this client, for a total of close to $20 million for computer equipment. All of this was done without having the assistant treasurer sign a commitment letter or make any formal gesture of approval. And all of it was done essentially because the salesman made it easy for the assistant treasurer to proceed with the series of transactions.

There are a number of lessons to be learned from this example. First is the importance of determining why prospects act as they do; second is the importance of meeting prospects' specific needs, however different they may be from the ordinary. In this case, the prospect had had a bad experience and was very fearful that it might be repeated. He was hesitant about signing anything. By showing trust in the prospect and not requiring the usual signed commitment letter, the salesman took a calculated risk that the prospect would return the confidence. The prospect was also fearful there would be some administrative or other problem which would cause him embarrassment. By working with the prospect every step of the way, the salesman allowed him to concentrate on the savings to his company rather than on possible problems. The mutual trust developed evolved into a long and satisfactory relationship.

This example also points out again the importance of determination. Although the prospect was initially abrupt and gruff, the salesman persevered. In effect, the prospect's gruff exterior frightened off all the competition, and the salesman's job was much easier.

Don't take no for an answer

Another salesman of my acquaintance had two rather unusual experiences which pointed up the same lesson. In the first instance, he was calling on a large company he thought should be a good prospect for his product, a somewhat unique form of compensation planning. The financial officer seemed rather doubtful but agreed to an interview. Because the salesman was convinced the company was a good prospect, he proceeded.

During this meeting the chief financial officer for the prospect disclaimed any interest in the product. The salesman, however, persisted in his contacts. When, six months later, the situation in the company changed dramatically, he obtained a substantial amount of business on a virtually noncompetitive basis. His competition had taken the chief financial officer's disclaimer at face value and had effectively withdrawn from competition. By persevering, the salesman not only obtained the business but obtained it virtually without competition.

In the second instance, the salesman telephoned for an interview. He was not given one, but he did have a long, pleasant, and informative chat with the president of the company. The salesman followed up on the conversation with a detailed written analysis on why he thought the company should use his product, although the president had told him they would never have use for it. Surprisingly, six months later the company's situation changed. The salesman was called to a meeting the Saturday before Easter and closed the entire transaction for a substantial amount of compensation the following Tuesday, again on a virtually noncompetitive basis.

This type of situation suggests several lessons to be learned. Sometimes companies fail to realize that they may *become* prospects. If you are convinced that they are or will become good prospects, you should maintain a low-key but persistent follow-up which will improve your understanding of their circumstances and their understanding of you and your product. Often prospects who are most emphatic in their denials of interest are also frightening away the competition, with the net effect of increasing your chances of success.

2 | Projecting the image of success

A person with the characteristics of intelligence, empathy, sympathy, and ego strength has the greatest chance of success in big-ticket financial sales. But merely having these characteristics is not enough; the salesperson must also project an image which is inoffensive to everyone and inspires confidence. The way a salesman of financial services talks and the way he looks often will determine whether he will ever get beyond the first contact.

HOW TO GET YOUR STORY ACROSS

No one can please everyone all the time, but a salesperson has to try. Some years ago I telephoned the president of a small southern textile company. We chatted, and it became apparent that, although his company did not require my product, they might in a few years. I said good-bye, sent the president a brief form letter, and marked the file to recontact him in about two years.

When, after two years, I telephoned him again I identified myself and my company. I was amazed at his response:

He: You called me before, didn't you?
Me: Yes sir, I did call you about two years ago, more or less.
He: Didn't I tell you then we don't need your product?
Me: Yes, you did, but that was two years ago, and the world keeps turning and changing, so I thought I'd check with you again.
He: That's the trouble with you fast-talking salesmen. You don't listen. You're pushy. All you fast-talking Yankees are the same.

To this prospect I was a fast-talking, high-pressure "Yankee" salesman, even though I was calling from Baltimore, which is well below the Mason-Dixon Line, and my approach was quite leisurely, perhaps even too low-keyed by some standards.

Developing a speaking technique which, if less than golden tongued, is at least not tongue-tied, requires empathy. Depending on the prospect or client, you may have to "machine gun" facts or approach your presentation as leisurely as you would a summer stroll. Both techniques may be used at different times with the same prospect. You let him set the tone of your discussion, or you react to his attitude in such a way as to arouse his interest, curiosity, greed, or other emotions.

The best speaker can be the worst salesman because he lacks knowledge of his product. A slow-speaking, knowledgeable expert can coax agreement from the most reluctant prospect by his sincerity and obvious grasp of the facts, despite a poor delivery.

Your best chance of success in speaking to others is to know yourself, your strengths and your weaknesses, and then to build on your strengths in conversation and learn to correct your weaknesses. By being yourself, a unique individual, you enhance your effectiveness because you will be relaxed and sincere. These are qualities that are going to sell; they should be showcased, just as an actor does.

Analysis of speaking ability

You can improve your speaking ability by analyzing it in different situations before a group, with an individual face to face, or using the telephone. Because it is difficult to rate yourself, the best way to do this is to make presentations of these types accompanied by an associate who will take notes, record your strengths and your weaknesses, and then critique you as soon as possible. After you have made the necessary improvements and corrections, the same associate should accompany you as you engage in the same types of encounters and then reexamine your performance using the same criteria.

In evaluating telephone sales technique, only one side of the conversation is available to the associate. This is usually enough to allow obvious flaws to be picked up, however. Telephone presentations can be followed with instant evaluation, which is most valuable in making corrections.

Depending on your expertise, it may take weeks or years before you feel fully confident speaking in any sales situation. The more experience you obtain, the more quickly you will be able to improve your techniques. Practice may not make perfect, but it always makes better.

To a great degree, your progress will depend on your mental attitude. If you view speaking to others as a painful chore, it will remain difficult. If you view it as an opportunity to enjoy yourself and to make money at the same time, you will find it much easier to improve.

If no associate is available to assist you, self-evaluation, although more difficult, is an alternative. It is important to quiz yourself as soon as possible after every speaking experience and to attempt to be completely objective. After every call you can rate yourself on a scale of 0–10 on your:

1. Ability to project your personality.
2. Eye contact.
3. Voice control.
4. Body movements and gestures.
5. Use of sales aids.
6. Content of the presentation.
7. Ability to answer questions and objections.
8. General audience reaction.

Whether you are working with an associate or evaluating yourself, you should make it a point to keep records on your weaknesses and strengths, suggested changes, and ratings. By comparing these periodically, you will be able to pinpoint areas of progress and areas which need more work.

Speaking techniques

You learn to develop the necessary speaking techniques by practice, by analyzing your successes and failures, and by continuing to learn as you work. Some techniques to assist you in being a more effective speaker are suggested here.

In person or on the telephone, it is generally better not to try to tell jokes. Even professional comedians bomb occasionally, and in telling jokes there is always the chance of offending someone or some group. Since you don't know your prospects' sensitivities, why risk offending them? Since you are not a professional comedian, why risk embarrassing yourself? Wry, self-deprecating remarks are sometimes useful, since they can't threaten your listener and they may indicate that you don't take yourself too seriously. They also allow you to express criticism of conventional wisdom in a pleasant way. Sarcastic remarks directed to others, however, are always out of place; they do only harm.

Most salespersons tend to speed up their speech as they become emphatic or excited. Learning to slow down, particularly for emphasis, is very necessary. A small card with the word *slow* printed on it to be carried with you into an interview or laid beside the telephone while calling can be helpful. If your listeners don't understand you, you might as well not be talking. In any complicated presentation it is important to check the listeners' reactions as you proceed. Do they understand? Go back over the salient points of your presentation. Do they agree? Ask for assent. The longer the presentation, the more important it is to repeat the salient points and check for understanding and agreement.

Varying the pitch and volume of your voice is the best way to indicate emphasis and keep the listener interested. Even the best speaker who has no change of pace can be boring. Dropping the volume to almost a whisper can be as effective as shouting. A drumbeat rhythm can be most emphatic.

In personal interviews with a single individual or speaking before a group, looking your audience in the eye is the only way to be sure of their attention. Eye contact is vital in retaining interest, and it indicates determination and sincerity. These are qualities you want to project.

A set, memorized presentation is usually not desirable. It may appear as if the message were "canned" and perhaps uncertain, and it often seems to lack sincerity. What you *should* memorize is a list of the salient features of your product and its presentation. Then you can deliver your presentation in a manner which suggests that it has been expressly prepared for the listener. You also avoid the problem of being interrupted in a memorized speech, and then perhaps being unable to gather your thoughts again and continue. Such a situation can be fatal to any sales presentation. If you really understand and know what you are attempting to say, you can welcome interruptions and still press on with your main points.

When speaking before a group, avoid a stationary position such as behind a lectern. Movement is necessary to maintain interest, as are gestures, and both are virtually useless if you are hiding behind something solid. Some public speakers grasp lecterns as if they were drowning and were afraid their last support was slipping from their grasp. Such a posture might inspire sympathy but not confidence in you, and that is what you are seeking. Gestures below the waist, which can give the appearance of uncertainty, hesitancy, and lack of confidence, should be avoided. To be certain the microphone is mobile and in working order and that any other equipment, such as speakers or projectors, to be used in a presentation to a group is operative, they should be tested well in advance.

Flip charts can be useful as an aid in explaining a complicated problem or its solution. They should not be used as a crutch or as a substitute for knowing your business. In using such charts, care must be taken to maintain eye contact and to vary the pitch and volume of voice. Other aids, such as projectors or movies, are good for presenting complex, visually oriented presentations before large groups. However, they lack spontaneity and may cause listeners' interest to drop off. In financial sales, I doubt that such charts or other aids should ever be used.

Using hand-held cue cards for any major or involved presentation, particularly before a group, is an absolute necessity, however. You need not try to hide them or apologize for them. Merely state that you have a lot of points to cover and data to present, and you want to be sure to be absolutely accurate. That is all that need be said. Such cards should be numbered to help you cover all major points in order. This also helps you see the trend of your thought should the cards become mixed. The cards should be printed large enough to be read without glasses (if you need them). You may want to remove your glasses to gesture, or it may be impractical for one reason or another to wear them. By using cue cards, you can be assured of giving a fully understood presentation which covers all the points, and you will still appear to be speaking in an impromptu manner.

In one-on-one, in-person interviews, you should try to be relaxed but not too relaxed, at ease but not sprawling. Generally, it is wise to let the prospect or client set the tone as far as small talk is concerned. In some parts of the country, such as the South and West, at least 15 minutes is needed for small talk, whereas in some of the major cities such as New York or Chicago, 3 minutes could be considered being overtalkative. In any event, getting to the point is never a mistake.

As in dealing with a group, eye contact is important, but it should not be challenging. Some people use the technique of looking at the other person's nose or mouth, rather than always looking directly at the eyes. It may be wise to look those in the eye who seem to welcome it, and glance only periodically at those who seem to be made uncomfortable by this practice.

Regardless of what other sales aids you may use in an interview, you should always have a large lined pad and pen available to illustrate your points or make computations. As you engage in more interviews, you will become more sensitive to the reaction you are receiving from the other party. Sometimes you will find that you are not receiving attention. This may be due to factors beyond your control, such as events that occurred directly before your meeting, or it may be due to the other person's disinterest in your product. Sometimes the best way to find out is to ask: "I'm getting the feeling that I'm not reaching you. Is there something I've missed?"

Talking over the telephone differs from direct interviews in several ways. Usually you will speak to a secretary first. It is wise to tell the secretary who you are, who you represent, and your purpose, so your call can be properly announced. Once you get to speak to your client or prospect you should have some point of interest ready to grasp his attention, since you may have less than 60 seconds to make an initial impact.

Compared to personal interviews, you are operating at a severe disadvantage in telephoned contacts because you may be calling

Projecting the image of success 23

at the wrong time and not realize it, and you can't see the other party's face and gain any reaction from it. You also can easily be cut off before you can obtain all the facts or tell your entire story. Thus an initial impact is much more important than it is in a face-to-face conversation. Before you place a call you should have some idea of what will interest the other party most, and you should be prepared to make this point as quickly as possible in your conversation. If the point is not made quickly, it may never be made. As Chapter 5, "Prospecting," notes, it is important to be both direct and brief in telephone conversations. It is seldom effective to make complete sales presentations by telephone.

In many cases you will be unable to reach the party you are calling on the initial call. The information you have given the secretary —your name, company, and the complete purpose of your call— should then be left as a message. In the event repeated calls are necessary to make contact, the accumulated weight of your calls assists you in getting through. If you have not left messages, every call is considered as if it were the first one.

Putting into practice these suggestions for improving your speaking ability may not make you a polished orator, but you should be able to hold your own in most of the sales situations you encounter. In any case, you will have laid the foundation for greater confidence and continuing improvement.

HOW TO LOOK THE PART

The way a salesperson looks obviously varies with the type of sales. If you are selling musical instruments, you may well look like a musician; if you are selling textbooks, perhaps you look like a professor. If you are selling financial services, it seems to make sense that you look like a business executive, stockbroker or banker, but you don't want to look like a musician or professor.

Being inappropriately dressed is a sure way to destroy the image of success and confidence the salesman of financial services must project. He must look like a businessman, not a racetrack tout or a rock group fan. Two-or-three button suits of conservative cut and fabric make the best impression and are least likely to go out of style. Following fads may be fun for leisure activities, but they are out of place in a business office where financial decisions are being made. They also are expensive and can leave owners with a substantial investment in clothing which soon becomes worthless.

Women entering the field of financial service sales must also dress conservatively and within the bounds of good taste. Presenting a businesslike appearance may be the best way to keep relations on the proper impersonal level with the men who make the buying decisions in most big-ticket sales. Women have somewhat more leeway than men do as far as colors and accessories are concerned, but basic fashions for women in business have taken on almost as rigid requirements as those for men. A tailored suit and a white or solid-colored blouse are the norm.

I don't feel qualified to give women advice on their clothing, but common sense should be their guide. Like men, women's clothing should be uniform in style and quality so that they consistently project a businesslike image.

Dressing according to plan

Most men buy their clothes haphazardly. They have no consistent style. They mix their colors, and the weights of their suits may be inappropriate. Particularly if you are starting your career or are at an early stage in it, it is important to get as much clothing as you can for your dollar.

A minimum wardrobe such as those suggested in the accompanying checklists represents a fairly substantial investment. But you can spend much more on clothes if you merely buy what you like with no overall plan. In such a case, no amount of money spent on a wardrobe can give you the assurance of always presenting the appearance of a well-dressed salesman.

Grey and blue are the suit colors most favored by businessmen; solid colors, muted stripes, small plaids, tweeds, and herringbones are generally preferred. Brown is much less popular, and other colors, broad stripes, or patterns are out.

Next to suits, shirts are probably the most important item in a man's wardrobe. A reasonably good quality shirt with the appropriate tie can greatly enhance the appearance of a relatively inexpensive suit. Tests have shown that new acquaintances' eyes usually are drawn first to a man's face and the triangle comprised of the shirt and tie, framed by the suit. Button-down, oxford-cloth

CHECKLISTS OF MINIMUM WARDROBES FOR SALESMEN OF FINANCIAL SERVICES

A minimum starting wardrobe for salesmen living and working where there is freezing weather in winter and the summers are warm but not excessively long might include:

- 3 winter-weight suits, blue or grey
- 3 midweight suits, blue or grey
- 9 white or blue long-sleeved, button-down, oxford-cloth shirts, wash and wear preferred
- 12 ties, regimental stripes, challis, or small figures
- 9 pairs knee-length socks, dark blue or grey
- 2 pairs winged-tip or moccasin-toe laced shoes
- 9 sets of underwear
- 12 white handkerchiefs
- 1 felt hat
- 1 rain hat
- 1 lined raincoat
- 1 pair of gloves
- 1 overcoat or storm coat
- 1 black or dark belt
- 1 scarf
- 1 folding umbrella
- 1 set of Totes

Salesmen living and working in an area where the winters are shorter and the summers are longer and hotter should consider the following suggested minimum starting wardrobe:

- 3 midweight suits, blue or grey
- 3 summer-weight suits, solids, stripes, or cords
- 6 white or blue long-sleeved, button-down, oxford-cloth shirts
- 6 white or blue short-sleeved, oxford-cloth shirts
- 12 ties
- 9 pairs lightweight, knee-length socks
- 2 pairs winged-tip or moccasin-toe laced shoes
- 9 sets of underwear
- 12 white handkerchiefs
- 1 felt hat
- 1 rain hat
- 1 belt

1 folding umbrella
1 set of Totes
1 lined raincoat
1 topcoat

For salesmen who live and work in an area where there is no real winter, the following starting wardrobe is suggested:

3 midweight suits
4 summer-weight suits, solids, stripes, or cords
3 white or blue long-sleeved shirts
9 white or blue short-sleeved shirts
15 ties
9 pairs lightweight, knee-length socks
2 pairs winged-tip or mocassin-toe laced shoes
12 sets of underwear
12 handkerchiefs
1 rain hat
1 lined raincoat
1 folding umbrella
1 set of Totes

shirts retain their appearance despite long, hard usage and keep both the collar and tie in place. A wash-and-wear cotton and polyester fabric is easy to care for and absorbs perspiration better than broadcloth. Most men have a great deal of difficulty matching striped, figured, or exotic-colored shirts with the proper suits and accessories. I have bought nothing but white and blue shirts for many years, and I estimate that the time I have saved by not having to agonize over matching the shirt properly and the number of occasions I have avoided looking ridiculous have more than compensated for any monotony.

The next most important item in most men's wardrobe is their ties, which should be purchased with the idea of matching their suits. Regimental stripes, small figures, or challis in maroon, blue, and white make attractive and versatile ties. Good ties have become extremely expensive, and the best way to get your money out of them is to buy them no more than $3\frac{1}{4}$ inches wide (preferably in the range of $2\frac{1}{2}$ to $2\frac{3}{4}$ inches). These ties will go in and out of style but should never be so far out as to make them obsolete.

A salesman's shoes must not only look businesslike but provide the comfort necessary to those who may spend an entire day on their feet. Many of the better shoes have leather soles and heels, which are slippery and completely unsuitable for walking on city streets or tile floors. Wing-tipped or moccasin-toe shoes of the best possible quality, with rubber heels and soles if at all possible, are best. I have found that the forward-thrust shoes may not be attractive as narrower shoes with hard soles, but they give excellent service for the money and are a good deal more comfortable. Like all good clothes, shoes require maintenance; they must be kept shined, and when the heels are obviously worn, they should be replaced.

Socks do show, and they should be chosen to complement the suit. Despite the availability of socks which go to the knee and stay up by themselves, some men's socks still droop around their ankles. I have never seen a man, however handsome and well built, whose shins were at all attractive.

Plain white handkerchiefs—no initials, no patterns, nothing fancy—are a necessary accessory. A folded handkerchief in the breast pocket of a suit looks good and provides a spare. Medium-width belts with simple gold or silver buckles are more comfortable than wide belts and large buckles, and they are less likely to make the wearer an object of humorous attention. Suspenders are unneeded and should not be worn unless the suit coat will never be removed. Vests are popular, and where they add a layer of warmth in winter they are practical. I find it ridiculous to see a vest worn with a summer-weight suit.

Wearing a hat, assuming it is reasonable looking, gives a more businesslike appearance. And hats are functional: They keep your hair dry when it is raining, they keep it in place when it is windy, and in cold weather they keep your head warm. I doubt the claim that wearing a hat makes a man bald, because I have seen any number of old gentlemen with excellent heads of hair wearing hats, and I have seen many youngsters who never wear a hat and are rapidly losing their hair.

If you are traveling, you eventually are going to encounter rain or snow. The best way to prevent appearing at an appointment looking like last week's wash after it had gone through the washer but before it got to the dryer is to buy a collapsible umbrella and a pair of Totes to cover your shoes. They are both easily carried and well worth the expense.

Probably the most practical coat for traveling is a lined raincoat. White, off-white, or tan may look better, but they are much less practical than navy or black. Storm coats are common in areas where most of the winter it is at or below freezing. In some parts of the country a topcoat is the best answer, since it is lightweight, provides enough protection in winter, and is a good deal dressier than a raincoat. In any case, a coat should not make you look like a foreign correspondent or Humphrey Bogart in *Casablanca,* or like a rock star who just came over from England. The simpler a coat is in style and color, the easier it is to match with other clothing.

Ways to economize

There are ways to have good-quality clothing and still save money. One way is to buy ahead, rather than, like most people, waiting until you need the clothes. It is, of course, less expensive to buy all types of standard, good-quality clothing on sale. A discount of 10 to 20 percent is an aftertax saving which is equivalent to a pretax return of 30 to 40 percent on your investment. You can't make this kind of return anywhere else.

On certain items, such as underwear, socks, and handkerchiefs, there often are quantity discounts. These things never go out of style, and you will need them the rest of your life. They don't deteriorate with time, so they can be stored indefinitely in a small space. In buying socks, it is a good idea to stick to one color and one brand so they will still be wearable if one sock of a pair is lost or wears out.

The best way to economize is to avoid fads. The greatest expense in clothing is incurred when an item is discarded long before it is worn out merely because it has gone out of style. Millions of leisure suits have been effectively discarded, not to mention tens of millions of shirts with french cuffs or exaggerated collar styles, and God knows how many superwide ties which will never see the light of day again.

Even shoes go through style cycles. Over the past few years we have seen boots that go up to the ankle, then to mid-calf, then up to the knee; buckles, both useful and ornamental; high heels;

superthick rubber soles; and various other eye-catching variations. Many of these were in and out of style long before the first pair of heels had to replaced. Unless you have money to waste, standard winged-tip, moccasin, or plain-toe shoes are your best bet. I have even seen a number of red and yellow shoes being worn by men recently; you can be sure these will be "in" today and "out" tomorrow.

Tips on traveling

Salespersons who travel always find it a challenge to continue to look businesslike after they have sat in a train, car, or airplane for hours. Packing and unpacking clothing several times in the course of a week also does not improve its looks.

You must learn to pack efficiently. This means learning to fold a suit so it can be carried in a suitcase or carry-on bag and suffer the least wrinkles. It means learning to fill every nook and cranny of a suitcase with small items to get the maximum clothing in it and keep the contents from shifting around.

In choosing luggage, any kind that can be carried on a plane is best. The time saved in obtaining luggage after a flight and the annoyance avoided if suitcases are lost make carry-on luggage greatly superior to types that must be checked. You should be able to travel for at least a week using what you can pack in a carry-on soft-side suitcase, a garment bag, and a large attaché case with a slim, flexible, envelope-type case inside. If you have connecting flights through the major airports, like Atlanta or Chicago, a small wheeled device such as airline personnel use to carry their luggage is an excellent investment.

If you must check your luggage, the heaviest plastic units are advisable. Buying soft-side luggage to be checked is playing Russian roulette with it, since even the plastic units, as hard as they are, will be dented and gouged with just a few trips. The American Tourister commercial in which the gorilla tries to bash their luggage may be an exaggeration, but some of the airlines seem to have someone almost as bad handling passengers' suitcases. A heavy luggage strap serves two purposes: It prevents your suitcase from opening should the locks break, and it is an easy way to identify your luggage as it comes off the plane. Buying expensive luggage, particularly soft-side bags, is a waste of money if you travel by plane. Furthermore, it is an invitation to theft as your luggage is carried around the baggage merry-go-rounds.

Travelers need to know how to maintain their clothing on the go. A time-tested method of getting the wrinkles out of a suit fairly quickly is to hang it up in the shower out of the path of the water and turn the faucet to as hot as it can go. Be sure the plug is out of the tub and allow the water to run 15 minutes full blast. Then turn off the water and let the suit hang for at least an hour in the steam. This works wonders for wool suits and is at least partially effective on mixed blends. Carry pants hangers with you and hang up all your clothes as soon as possible after you arrive.

A final suggestion

Everyone likes to deal with healthy, happy-looking people. Salespersons must train for this profession just as if they were athletes. Obtaining sufficient rest and exercise and eating a plain diet are not options, they are musts. Selling requires a high energy level. Unhealthy or tired people can't maintain the pace necessary to be successful.

If you should be so unfortunate as to be chronically ill, you should give up the thought of being a salesperson if any other profession is open to you. If you are in good health but are intent on destroying yourself through overindulgence in food or drink, this is not the business for you, either. If you will treat your body with even the consideration you would give a new car, you should be able to maintain the energy and stamina required for success in this field.

3 | Selling is a state of mind

There is a tendency these days to blame everything unfortunate, from lower back pain to migraine headaches, on the negative effects of the mind on the body. We hear less often about the good that can come from thinking positive things. Perhaps this is merely a sign of the times. I can offer no professional help for lower back pain or headaches, but I do feel qualified to comment on the positive effects your frame of mind can have on your ability to sell.

THE NATURE OF SELLING

To understand how to approach selling with the proper frame of mind, you have to understand the nature of selling.

Selling consists, first, of making the first move toward another person. This is very difficult for some people to do; they are unable even to dial the number of a stranger at the other end of the telephone. The need to take the initiative may make these people cringe, or they may feel in their hearts, if not their minds, that such an advance is embarrassing or demeaning. They may be afraid of rejection or feel that selling lessens their status or self-worth.

Like many other salesmen of financial services, I make such calls without a quiver and enjoy doing so. We welcome new challenges, don't fear rejection, and are never embarrassed about it. We view such contact work as a golden opportunity to make a great deal of money while having a certain amount of fun.

The differences between the way these two types of people approach the tasks of prospecting and selling mark the difference between a good salesman (type A) and an unsuccessful one (type B). The characteristics of these two types are listed in the accompanying box.

CHARACTERISTICS OF TWO TYPES OF SALESMEN

Type A: A *Good* Salesman

1. Knows virtually everything about the product that can be learned.
2. Knows in intimate detail how the product can be useful to a prospect.
3. Feels confident of the product's value.
4. Has a basically optimistic view of life and what he is doing. Is sure of success.
5. Because of this optimism, takes a very positive approach. Asks the question, "How much do you want?" rather than "Do you want any?"
6. Doesn't fear rejection, doesn't feel embarrassed if rebuffed, and persists in the face of such rejection.
7. Is determined to succeed.

Type B: An *Unsuccessful* Salesman

1. Has gaps in knowledge of the product. Doesn't fully understand all its features.
2. Is basically unsure of various ways the product can help a prospect and is thus easily deterred by objections.
3. Lacks confidence in the product and as a result lacks confidence in ability to sell it.

Selling is a state of mind 33

> 4. Is basically pessimistic about life and, particularly, about what he is doing, and thus is programmed to fail.
> 5. Because of this pessimism, takes a negative approach with prospects. Is really asking, "You don't want any, do you?"
> 6. Is acutely fearful of rejection, feels embarrassed if it occurs, and so gives up quite easily.
> 7. Feels destined to fail.

Second, selling consists of finding a need to be filled. Simple, isn't it? Yet millions of salesmen never rise above mediocrity because they don't fully know their products, and they cannot practice the magic art of questioning and listening to their prospects to discover needs and show how the product can fill those needs. This will be more fully covered in Chapters 4 and 5.

Third, selling consists of filling prospects' perceived needs. Many salesmen fail because they try to sell prospects things or services the prospects don't need or want. Perhaps more commonly, they fail because they attempt to sell products or services the prospects do not *perceive* as needed or wanted. This facet of selling will be covered more fully in Chapters 5 and 6.

Fourth, selling consists of seeing a transaction through to its finish. This means obtaining the down payment, signing the contract, or whatever it takes to finally close a sales transaction. If you make the original contact with the prospect, find the prospect's need, fill the need, and then stop, you are going to be a very hungry and frustrated salesman. Every transaction must be seen through to its finish. You get paid only for finalizing and closing transactions. Many salesmen are like bashful grooms. They bring their sweethearts to the altar and then run out of courage before the final vows are said. We will talk about this more in Chapter 10.

Five, selling consists of servicing customers after they have purchased a product. This is covered in Chapter 11. Love them and leave them may be good advice for a sailor, but not for you.

FIRST THINGS FIRST

Suppose you are an abject, cringing, fearful, trembling type B salesman. Somewhere in that pitiful wreck you are there is a small spark that is sending out a message: "I want to be type A." Is it possible? It should be; after all, a beautiful butterfly can burst from a dull cocoon.

We start with those things we know you can do. First, get to know your product. The world's greatest salesman would know everything about what he is selling, as described in Chapter 4. Very simply, this requires studying, studying, studying. Then, learn *all* the ways your product can be useful to a prospect. If you don't know why a prospect should buy the product, how can you expect the prospect to know? Again, this requires study.

These are the things that anyone can do, and they are relatively easy. The more difficult part has to do with your frame of mind in approaching a prospect. I suggest adopting an optimistic view, not only about business but about life in general.

The rationale for optimism starts with some very basic premises. You may or may not believe in an afterlife. If you do believe that there is life after death, then certainly anything that happens to you in this life is relatively unimportant when compared with eternity. How, then, can you be fearful of embarrassment or failure? Even death becomes unimportant when viewed in the context of an unlimited future.

But even some people who profess to be religious essentially live their lives as if everything ended on the day of their death. Those who believe that everything ends with death have all the more reason to make the best of a short life. Surely they have more reason not to waste time and effort in worrying. Nothing that may happen to them can compare with the final event, which is the complete end of everything.

Whatever your reason, if you can adopt a basically optimistic philosophy of life it will be easier for you to make the most of what you have. Overcoming problems most people find difficult to face is easier when you expect to succeed. You automatically lose the fear of rejection or embarrassment when you put these fears in the context of a long-range view of where you are going and how you are getting there.

Therefore, regardless of whether you believe in an afterlife or not, I believe your creed should be: "Life is short, I will do my best, and I will fear nothing." Simplistic? Yes. Does it work? Yes, it does, at least it has for me and for many salesmen I have trained.

To enhance your mental attitude before attempting to sell anything to anyone, whether in person or over the telephone, tell yourself:

1. I am financially independent. I have a million dollars in T bills.
2. I know all there is to know about my product.
3. I am selling the best product in the market.
4. I am the world's greatest salesman!
5. I am doing this prospect a favor in calling on him.

Note the five I's. This is not a game for the humble.

You may think, "I don't have a million dollars in T bills or anything else. I have $42 in the bank, and I am making car payments, and my mortgage payments are two months behind. I am not the world's greatest salesman; I may not be a salesman at all. I *don't* know my product very well, and it may not be the best product in the market and, to be honest, I am not sure who is doing whom the favor." My reply to you is: It makes no difference, if you can *act* as if all this were true. Walk into your prospect's office with a spring in your walk, vibrating with energy and sincerity, head high, and with determination in your eyes. You have everything to gain. You have nothing to lose.

FROM LOSER TO WINNER

Some years ago, an acquaintance of mine with a number of years' experience in various types of financial sales decided to sell life insurance. After working for a number of companies, with diminishing results, he ended up with a company selling debit life insurance. In selling this type of life insurance, the salesman solicits door to door and collects the premiums either weekly or monthly. My acquaintance has a snapshot of himself dressed in baggy trousers in which he is dejected looking, slouching, and clutching his debit book. The picture was taken in a grimy parking lot outside a rundown diner.

Shortly after this picture was taken, he obtained a reprieve with an opportunity to sell rather sophisticated financial services to major corporations. Because this work entailed meeting the treasurers and financial vice presidents of major companies, he spent his last dollars on a decent pair of shoes, a couple of suits, and a new overcoat. Today, many years later, he is one of the more successful people in the industry. He has had the snapshot enlarged and enclosed in plastic, and it has a place of honor on his desk. He has also given it a title—"The Loser." He says he keeps it as a reminder of less fortunate days.

Recently, I asked him what had changed a loser into a winner in his case. He told me this:

> I spent every waking hour learning about my product. I wanted to know everything that pertained to it, and I am continuing to learn about it today. As a result of this study, I decided that I knew my product as well as anyone in the world. Certainly, I knew more about it than any of those people to whom I was attempting to sell it.
>
> Before every day's prospecting, I had a talk with myself. I told myself that I was the world's greatest salesman and that I was doing these people a substantial service in sharing my knowledge with them. Somehow this talk buoyed me up and gave me real confidence. This attitude seemed to come through to those I dealt with. Soon I began to enjoy real success, and my confidence increased even further. When difficulties arose, I asked myself what the world's greatest salesman would do in this case. Whatever the answer, I had usually failed to do it. When I began to attempt to *act* like the world's greatest salesman, I came close to becoming one.

Today this man, 20 years older than in the picture, stands straight and radiates enthusiasm, knowledge, and confidence. Clearly, his attitude and frame of mind have had a very positive effect.

PLAYING THE GAME TO WIN

My years of selling and training salesmen have convinced me that the average salesman never realizes a fraction of his potential because of his inhibitions. He is afraid to shock or offend a prospect, afraid to go "all out" for a sale. He is afraid of rejection, afraid of embarrassment. Essentially, he is afraid of success.

If you have the qualities of a successful salesman defined in Chapter 1—intelligence, empathy, sympathy, and ego strength—you can learn to be a great salesman. A simple way to do this is to

Selling is a state of mind

think what a great salesman should be doing in every instance and then act it out. By acting out what should be done, you are training yourself to be what you want to be.

If your frame of mind can give you a backache or a headache, surely it should be able to give you the incentive and the means to be what you want to be. If you approach your work as a challenge to find the best possible ways of prospecting and selling, you will find out that instead of hard work it is almost a game. Further, it is a game you can always enjoy because you are improving at it, and it pays very well.

To win in this game requires energy and will power. My tested and proven method of developing and increasing these attributes involves keeping fit and getting in the proper frame of mind. Some proven ways of keeping fit are:

1. Engage in some form of physical activity for at least one hour every day, such as walking, jogging, or swimming. These rhythmical forms of exercise develop your heart and lung capacity and build energy levels. I consider tennis to be a skill game on a par with shooting pool, and golf, as a form of exercise, as a joke at best. Get out and sweat. Use your muscles, develop your wind. You will feel better.

2. Try to average seven or eight hours of sleep a night. You will not only feel better, you will look better.

3. Watch your diet. Take a vitamin supplement if you need one. Smoking is a form of suicide, and too much booze is almost as bad. If moderation was good for the ancient Greeks, it should be good for you.

4. If you have any doubts about your health, resolve them by having a complete physical examination. It is worth the cost if it resolves any anxiety you may have.

If you follow these suggestions you should be looking and feeling better every day. Some ways to get in the proper frame of mind for prospecting and selling are:

1. Face facts. Look at your beliefs and extend them to their logical conclusions. Determine to act as if you *really* believe what you say you believe. Change your beliefs if you can't live with the old ones, but, above all, determine to act in a manner consistent with what you *do* believe.

2. Examine your own worth. Compare yourself with your peers. You could get a pleasant surprise. Just being reasonably active and healthy will put you ahead of many of them.

3. Determine to act. Determine to move toward your goal, whatever it may be. Assume you will be sometimes right and sometimes wrong, but at least you will always be making progress.

4. Don't be afraid to fail. As a general, George Washington lost more battles than he won, but he won the last ones. Many great businessmen have failed before they succeed. The difference between ultimate success and ultimate failure is often no more than trying one more time. Remember, what any man has done, you can do.

5. When in doubt as to how to act, make a decision and don't look back.

6. Remember every day is another opportunity to enjoy life. Don't waste it!

4 | What to do before the first interview

If you act on the belief that you are the world's greatest salesman, as suggested in Chapter 3, you cannot afford to be lazy. You will recognize the worth of the suggestion by Helmuth Graf von Moltke, a German general, that troops should "train hard, fight easy." In big-ticket financial sales, this advice makes a great deal of sense. You must learn all you can about your product, both specifically and generally, long before you make your first contact. Your goal is to know more about your speciality than your prospects do—a lot more.

BUILDING A KNOWLEDGE BASE

Before you can begin to sell big-ticket financial services, you have to build a background of theoretical and practical knowledge. If you do not have an undergraduate degree in business administration, finance, economics, accounting, or a similar discipline, you have a long road to travel. You can take these courses exclusively or enroll in a school with the idea of obtaining a degree.

Unless you are past 40, I suggest trying for the degree. Its value lies not only in what you learn in obtaining it but in how prospective employers view you. Many positions require candidates to have such a degree even to be considered, much less actually be hired. If you have an MBA, you are ahead of most of your competition.

What to look for in *The Wall Street Journal*

Regardless of your technical background, it is necessary to stay informed about the current financial scene. One way to do this is to at least skim *The Wall Street Journal* every day. Knowing what to look for will help you get the most value out of the time you spend this way.

The front page of the *Journal* has six columns. The column on the far left usually is some general-interest story which may or may not have financial overtones. The next two columns, under the heading "What's News," are business and finance stories and worldwide summaries. These columns summarize the most important news events occurring in the previous 24 hours. The fourth column usually includes some sort of financial chart and a general-interest story. The next column, second from the right, is usually devoted to some special topic of interest, such as taxes or a study of the economy. The last column on the right generally is a story on some topic of economic interest. The entire front page should be skimmed, and the two columns under "What's News" should be read in full.

Throughout the paper there is a variety of items which may be interesting or useful. Roughly midway is the editorial page, which also has articles of general interest and book reviews. The want ads often make as interesting reading as the financial section, since they indicate in some detail which companies are hiring and the positions they are seeking to fill. They also give a fairly good idea of general salary levels. At least occasionally you will see your speciality listed there.

The "Who's News" section gives information on management changes, and a digest of earnings reports details the most recently reported quarterly, semiannual, and annual earnings of public companies. Just skimming these sections for familiar names can provide many interesting tidbits of information. The stockholder meeting briefs, concise one- or two-paragraph summaries of the stockholder meetings of major corporations, should be examined closely for names of your customers or competitors.

A section called "Financing Business" is concerned with new issues of stocks and bonds. If your specialty has anything to do with any form of financing through common stocks or bonds, this section should be studied very closely. A small box called "Prices of Recent Issues" lists recent bond offerings with their terms and current yields. Monitoring this box is an excellent way to keep abreast of long-term money rates. There are also boxes showing the asset values of a number of closed end mutual funds and a number of current tax-exempt bonds and their prices. A section called "Credit Market" has to do with the current situation in new debt offerings.

The box titled "Money Rates" is one of the most important sections of the *Journal,* even though it is very small. It lists the following rates: U.S. prime rate, federal funds rate, discount rate, call money rate, two commercial paper rates, a number of CD rates, and banker's acceptance rates. It also lists Eurodollar rates, foreign prime rates, T-bill rates, and various others. Here in one little section, one column wide and perhaps 6 inches long, you can find a summary of what is happening in the financial markets all over the world.

There are sections on commodities, futures, smaller exchanges, asset value of various open-end mutual funds, option quotations, government securities prices, government agencies' securities prices, over-the-counter common stock quotes, and the American and New York Stock Exchange prices of the preceding day. Also listed is the foreign exchange rate for most of the world's currencies. A series of charts shows the Dow Jones industrial averages. Information is given on daily percentage leaders on the New York Stock Exchange, New York Stock Exchange highs and lows, and other stock market reports. The last page of each issue is devoted to some topic of general interest related to finance or taxes.

Depending on your particular specialty, you will find various parts of the *Journal* of greater interest than others. Should your interest have anything to do with economic affairs outside the United States, a subscription to *The Financial Times,* which is comparable to *The Wall Street Journal* and published in London, or *The Economist,* another British periodical, would be a good investment.

I have found that it is a good idea to note in a small ring binder the information from the *Journal* which is of greatest interest to you. For instance, if your specialty is chiefly concerned with changing money rates, you might jot down the prime rate, the CD rate, and the federal funds rate periodically and keep track of their changes in direction. If your interests have anything to do with commodities, you might keep track of their prices in your notebook at least once a week. If your specialty requires knowledge of foreign exchange, changes in the foreign capital exchange rates and foreign prime rates might be noted. Whatever your area of interest, it pays to keep some written record of the items you are checking. A month or a year later, you can come back and see what trends have been developing.

Other general information sources

Residents of cities such as New York, Chicago, Los Angeles, or San Francisco have an excellent source of information in their local newspapers. If you live in a city without a good daily paper, you probably should be receiving, at least on a weekly basis, the newspaper of the nearest major city. Financially oriented publications such as *Fortune, Forbes,* and *Barron's* can be very useful in broadening your general outlook if you skim them for the areas in which you have the most interest. They also are valuable in examining your specialty.

With any of these publications, it is important to get into the habit of at least skimming every issue. The world is changing constantly, and only constant attention will give you anything like an accurate picture.

You may be surprised at the amount of information to be found in a public library. Most city libraries include complete sets of Moody's stock reports, as well as the Standard and Poor's reports. They usually have current copies of *The Wall Street Journal* and other financial publications.

There also are books related to almost every financial specialty. You should make an attempt to read one of these every month or so and outline it chapter by chapter as you go. This accomplishes

What to do before the first interview

two things. It increases your comprehension and allows you to retain a great deal more of the information, and it allows you to go back and review the material you have read much more easily. If the book is borrowed, your notes are your only source available for later reference.

GATHERING INFORMATION ON PROSPECTS AND COMPETITORS

Even if you have a strong base of general information about financial affairs, you must learn all you can about your prospects.

If the prospect is an individual, this information can be difficult to obtain. You can check the Dun and Bradstreet list of corporate directors, look at available public information on the prospect's employer or company, and, of course question associates.

If the prospect is a publicly held corporation, it must submit information to the Securities and Exchange Commission on Form 10K annually and Form 10Q quarterly. Publicly owned corporations also usually supply information to Standard and Poor's or Moody's. They generally issue quarterly and annual corporate reports, some of which are quite lengthy. These reports provide information of a financial nature and other details on the business. Questioning a prospect's competition also can be very informative.

In the case of a privately held corporation where no public information is available, the only source of information available may be statistics on the industry as a whole. This can allow you to arrive at a fairly good "guesstimate" of the overall situation of some prospects.

Some years ago I was calling on a large privately owned textile company in North Carolina. While I was waiting for my appointment, I browsed through an industry journal which featured a statistical study that included employment, sales, and profit totals for a number of major publicly owned corporations. The company I was calling on supplied only employement information to Dun and Bradstreet, so I averaged the publicly owned companies' data to obtain probable sales and profit figures on my prospect.

During my interview with the financial officer, I mentioned my best guess as to their sales and profits. This company's results must have been almost precisely on the statistical average, because he became quite upset and wanted to know where I had obtained my information. It was obvious he felt that I had somehow obtained confidential information. When I told him how I had arrived at my guess, he rushed from the office, got the journal, came back, and immediately verified my computations. Obviously, I had hit very close to the mark.

In addition to knowing about the economy and your prospects, knowing the competition is essential if you are to beat them. It is extremely valuable to know precisely what your competition is doing and why they are doing it. I find that the best source of information on the competition, aside from published materials, is firsthand reports. These can be obtained by questioning prospects who have either done business with them or been solicited for sales by them and individuals who are looking for employment, are now working, or have worked for the competition.

A professional salesman makes it a point never to speak ill of his competition. He can, however, tell the truth, and 100 percent of the truth. Be very careful never to say anything about your competitors that you would not want to repeat in front of one of their representatives. You may find that if you speak ill of them, that is precisely what you will be doing in a court of law.

As with gathering information on prospects, industrywide data on competitors can help you make a general estimate of a particular company's situation.

PREPARING TO PROCEED

All this study accomplishes several purposes. It gives you an appreciation of the general business climate. You have to have a feel for the economy, interest rates, stock prices, commodity prices, and other factors affecting the overall economic climate in general and your industry in particular.

You also should know the outlook for your prospects and competitors and how they are affected by current events. Knowledge of your prospects enables you to tailor your product or sales presentation to their needs. Knowing your competition, what they are doing and why, enables you to meet them better.

Studying the sources suggested here should improve your ability to point up the advantages of your product in relation to changes in the environment which affect your prospects. The highest accolade you can receive as a salesman is to be told that you know your business better than any of your competition. If you are well prepared, every interview is easy and, usually, productive.

Following this advice can help you change yourself from a fumbling amateur into a polished professional. You know how to present the appearance of a trim-figured, confident, well-dressed, well-spoken individual. With the added dimension of a broad knowledge of the economic scene, your prospects and products, and your competitors, you should be ready to venture into the world and commence prospecting for sales.

5 | Prospecting

If we were to question 100 salespersons or prospective salespersons about the aspect of selling they like the least, the chances are that 99 of them would answering "prospecting." This is why so many help-wanted advertisements for salespersons specify "no prospecting required."

Why is prospecting perceived to be so difficult? I think it is because most salespersons don't know *how* to prospect. In addition, their attitude is such that they are almost beaten before they start. A feeling of extreme frustration results from half-heartedly attempting to do something that they know they are mishandling.

FINDING THE HIDDEN TREASURE

The purpose of this chapter is to outline in general and specific terms how to prospect successfully and how to enjoy it. If you mold your body, mind, and will so that you welcome new challenges, you should be prepared to view prospecting as an opportunity, not a chore.

I like to think of prospecting as walking down a beach with a metal detector. I know there are coins and valuable jewelry lost in the sand. I have the equipment to find them. I require only determination and patience to garner a rich reward. In the meanwhile, I am out in the fresh air receiving beneficial exercise. If you can view prospecting with the same positive attitude, you will find it is enjoyable.

This book is designed to assist all sellers of big-ticket financial services. There are essentially two types of these services, and the methods of prospecting for sales in them are quite different. The types are:

1. Financial services aimed primarily at individuals, such as tax shelter sales, life insurance, mutual funds, stocks and bonds, commodities, and tax planning and asset planning services.
2. Financial services designed principally for the use of corporations of various sizes, such as pension planning and benefit plans, investment banking, acquisition service, bank and insurance company lending, equipment leasing and financing, corporate financing, and consulting.

PROSPECTING FOR INDIVIDUAL SALES

Prospecting aimed at individuals is usually limited to persons in a given area, such as a city, county, or possibly an entire state. It involves discovering who may be interested in buying the product, how buyers can be separated from nonbuyers, and how to make the most effective sales approach.

The way to begin is by examining the individuals who are presently buying the product. Then determine from whom they are buying it, why they are buying it, and why are they buying it from the present sellers. If you know these things, you can attempt to discover what you can offer that is better, different, less expensive, easier to buy, more prestigious, faster, or in any way more appealing.

As an example, we will use a specific product, security sales to individuals. Suppose you represent a regional stockbroker in a medium-size eastern city. Your area includes a number of major New York Stock Exchange firms located within the city or within

Prospecting 49

easy travel distance. Your task is to set up a prospecting plan. How should you go about it?

Step 1

Step 1 is to determine who will be your best prospects. This can be done by analyzing your present client list or using a demographic study done by the New York Stock Exchange, the U.S. Bureau of the Census, or another fact-finding group. Common sense would indicate that your best prospects are persons over 21 years of age with either extra income beyond that necessary to maintain their lifestyles or inherited wealth. Women probably outnumber men as owners of various types of securities because they often outlive their husbands. Owners of businesses, executives, professional persons, and others in high income brackets should be your best prospects.

The Census Bureau makes statistics available on average family incomes in different areas. Usually they are compiled on the basis of postal zip codes, which makes it easy to pinpoint where such people live.

Step 2

Step 2 is to determine from whom your prospects are presently buying securities. This is probably local or nearby brokerage houses, although some may deal with major city firms. Others may be buying through local or other banks or trust departments.

Step 3

You must now ask yourself why people buy securities. On the basis of experience with your personal client list, you would find that most security buyers fall into several easily recognizable categories. These include:

1. Conservative purchasers who buy principally to preserve capital or to develop income. Individuals in this group normally buy certain types of conservative common stocks and are apt to own preferred stock, bonds, or mutual funds.

2. Aggressive investors who are principally interested in long-term capital gains. They are usually more interested in ownership of individual common stocks.
3. Speculators who are interested in both long- and short-term capital gains. They normally own common stocks, warrants, and bonds at certain times in the interest cycle. At various times they may also own options or commodity positions.
4. Buyers who buy securities for corporate purposes or enter the commodity markets to hedge against risk entailed in their normal businesses.

Step 4

The next step is to determine why these individuals are buying securities and other types of investments from their present sources. I doubt if there is a great deal of statistical information available on this. However, your common sense and experience elsewhere will probably help.

You can start with the assumption that purchasers of something as important as investment advice and services will buy from people they know and feel comfortable with, or from strangers who are well known by reputation. In addition, all other things being equal, purchasers will probably give business to someone they like.

Within these guidelines, it is fairly reasonable to assume that a prospect who is presently dealing with a broker is doing so for one or more of the following reasons:

1. The broker is either a friend or a relative.
2. The firm is known by reputation.
3. The firm was recommended by a member of the family, a friend, the prospect's bank, or some other respected information source.
4. The prospect has been influenced by advertising over a period of time. Examples of effective advertising are the television spots featuring Merrill Lynch's stampeding bulls and E. F. Hutton's advice eavesdroppers.
5. The final possibility is easy access. Some prospects will deal with someone close by, even though there is no other reason to do so.

Step 5

Having determined why your prospects are dealing with the competition, you now must determine what, if anything, you can offer that will be appealing to them and may not now be offered by their connection. In the case of securities and related investment vehicles, it is very doubtful that you can offer any major price concessions, except to the most active traders. Commissions are no longer set by the New York Stock Exchange, and there are some firms that deal strictly in executing orders and offering commission price concessions. But an investment client who is looking for service cannot expect such price concessions. What is more important, you will probably not be able to offer them.

You can, however, offer more service. You and your firm may be able to do a number of things better than your prospects' present stockbrokers.

One thing is to offer more appropriate advice by making it a practice to get to know your prospects' resources and aspirations better than their present suppliers do. You certainly should be able to give prospective clients a feeling of greater importance than they are presently enjoying, and this feeling alone may be enough to win at least part of their business. We seem to be living in an era where many companies and many salespersons have altered the adage "The customer is always right" to "The customer is always wrong." As a result of this attitude and the general deterioration in quality of most manufactured products, anyone who really attempts to understand and meet a prospective customer's requirements will enjoy an advantage over competition.

It may be possible, either through your own research or that of your firm, to provide better or different information than your prospects are receiving. Every brokerage firm and advisory service seems to make this claim. In my experience, brokers who ignore stereotyped investment advice and make up their own minds about a specific strategy and timing are most successful over a period of time.

When I was a beginner in the brokerage business, I asked an older, more experienced, and very successful producer what advice he could give me to enhance my chances of success. Since my family had no money and my friends were not in a position to help me, I had to build my customer base from nothing, completely of strangers. The broker's advice was that if I would merely try to be 100 percent honest, I would enjoy the benefits of being "an original." He meant more than being honest in the sense of not taking anyone's money; he also suggested I must be intellectually honest with myself and my clients.

My efforts to act on this advice, unfortunately, consisted principally of admitting my mistakes. No one likes to do this, and when you are young admitting mistakes is particularly difficult. You have not built up enough confidence in your own abilities to take a series of setbacks easily. In the securities business, however, particularly when dealing in the speculative side of the market, it is imperative to cut your losses. By implication, this means admitting your mistakes.

Although I certainly was not 100 percent successful in following this excellent advice, I diligently attempted to do so. One time, particularly, it probably saved my clients and myself a great deal of money. Brunswick Corporation was riding the crest of the bowling craze; it was trading in the high 60s and appeared to be heading well into the 100s. I had been in and out of the stock several times, so I purchased it for my own account and induced a number of clients to go back in again in the high 60s. Within a week, the stock appeared to have topped. While it was very painful to recommend selling in such a short time, at very substantial losses, I got out myself and got all of my customers out in the 63–64 range. Hindsight proved that this was one of the best sales I ever made, because the stock began an almost uninterrupted descent to around 10. Had I failed to admit the mistake, not only would I personally have lost a great deal of money, but many of my clients would undoubtedly have become so alienated that no future business would have come from them.

In dealing with more conservative investments, these difficult decisions are, of course, much less frequent. Yet a diligent and honest broker dealing with those who customarily purchase bonds would have advised taking a loss if he had felt that the prime rate was going to go substantially above 12 percent during the early part of 1980. He might well have advised taking losses in some bonds, going into short-term paper, and holding funds to repurchase at lower prices. The alternative would have been to confirm his original purchase recommendations and recommend holding for better times. Again, the more honest approach would have been more profitable for the client and more difficult for the broker.

In determining if you are in a position to offer these or other services, it is wise to analyze your firm's resources and your own. Some individuals are better suited for speculation than others. If you are one of those who find making rapid decisions difficult or admitting mistakes agonizing, then you probably should confine yourself to the more conservative areas of investment. If, however, you enjoy working under intense pressure and making rapid decisions, and you have enough confidence in your ability so that you will be unshaken by mistakes, then you may be able to handle more speculative accounts. Whichever category you fall in, you should determine what services you and your firm can provide that may be appealing to a prospective client.

Step 6

Having deduced the reasons why prospects are dealing with their present stockbrokers, you must now develop a strategy to supplant, at least in part, these relationships. What do you do when a prospect states that he is now dealing with another firm because his Uncle Charles works there, or his friend George is his stockbroker, or it was recommended by his bank, or it has a national reputation much bigger than your firm's, or it is just closer? Your approach should be a very simple one:

> Frankly, Mr. Prospect, I don't know if you should be doing business with me. If we can get together for 15 minutes or a half hour, at your convenience, after the close of the market, maybe I can find out a little more about you and give you some idea what, if anything, we can do which would be helpful to you.

Note that you are suggesting a meeting after market hours. Even if you have not written a single order, you want to appear busy. At this meeting, you inquire about the prospect's objectives, resources, and present holdings. Most important, you want to find out what he is most unhappy with in his present connection. This should suggest a blueprint for doing better. Your approach then can be:

> Why not try doing part of your business with me, until you have a chance to compare? If I can do better for you, then I have earned your business; if I can't, you have done nothing but lose a little time.

Some people will rebuff your suggestions, but others will admire your aggressiveness, and these are the people who will provide your best sources for new business. In addition, a certain number of people will be unhappy with some facet of their present arrangement, and these will also provide new business.

Sources of individual prospects

Among the questions asked most often in sales meetings are: "How do I find names of people to contact? Where do I get my prospects?"

In selling such services as securities to individuals, a number of sources can be very useful. For example, Dun and Bradstreet publishes various directories of corporations and their officers, and most states and some cities and counties publish directories of all businesses in their areas. Such directories usually indicate type of business and number of employees and give some idea of sales and profits for each firm. In addition, they may list the top officers and directors. The U.S. Government Printing Office publishes various studies by the Bureau of the Census showing family income and various economic areas broken down by postal zip codes.

All of these would be useful in selling securities to individuals. In addition, if you are recommending investment in a specific stock or a certain industry, the yellow pages of your local telephone book will give you the names of the companies' local facilities or their competitors. Either may be a good source of new business.

Another source of business, often overlooked, is referrals. Salesmen who habitually ask every contact as well as every client for referrals usually have a constant stream of prospects' names coming in. Visiting accountants and attorneys to ask for their help is another commonly used tactic.

Advertising in financial journals and newspapers and on radio or television can, of course, be very useful. Traditionally, advertising in the security business has consisted of offering to mail prospects reports of research done on various companies or industries. A new wrinkle might be to advertise personalized advice sessions to be held by appointment after market hours. Such sessions allow possible investors to visit you at your office at a mutually convenient time to discuss their objectives and resources, as noted above. Another device might be to develop a telephone hot line you would operate one or two evenings a week for the same purpose.

Another method of meeting prospects is to give lectures, either in a facility you provide yourself or at local schools or stock clubs, women's clubs, and other such sites. Conducting regular or night school courses has also proven to be a good source of new contacts.

Your general objective must be to present as high a profile as possible and still maintain a professional demeanor. The demands on your time cannot interfere with your required presence in your office during market hours.

Cold calls can find hot prospects

Aside from the service you can perform for a prospect, what you are really selling is yourself. Some years ago I joined a major New York Stock Exchange firm as a registered representative. I knew nothing of the security business, had never even read *The Wall Street Journal*, and had no friends or family who could possibly be interested in buying any form of investments. Put succinctly, I started from absolute ground zero.

Up to that point, the most I had ever earned in any year was $5,520. In order to go into the security business, I had to accept employment at an annual starting salary of $4,800. Since I was married with two children, I was under a great deal of pressure to become successful as soon as possible.

After my initial training in New York, I returned to Baltimore. For a week or two I sat at my desk doing nothing much but reading current periodicals and following up on a few prospects who had been given to me by the firm. These had originated from answers to various advertisements offering specific stock reports and studies.

Then I began to realize that at my present pace, it would probably be several years before I began to earn as much as I had before entering the security business. When I sought guidance as to how to bring in business, no one was able to give me any real idea of how to proceed. I decided on a direct approach. Next to the public telephones in a drugstore across the street from our offices a city directory was kept. For a time I went over every day, purchased a cup of coffee, and stayed for an hour or two copying the names and addresses of nearby companies and their officers, if they were listed. After accumulating a number of names of prospects within walking distance, I began a systematic canvass of small businesses located within five miles of our office. Since I had no clients, I did not have to be concerned about losing office time. Every morning I went out about 10:00 A.M. and began my "cold calling."

As I look back, I cringe at the thought of my clumsiness and naiveté. Not only did I know nothing of selling, I also knew very little about the security business. But the idea of a relatively well-dressed stockbroker cold calling was then something of a novelty in Baltimore, as I imagine it is today, and a number of people, mostly the presidents of small companies, were kind enough to at least hear my story. I was asking them to give me a chance to make recommendations, and, if those recommendations proved useful, to give me part of their business.

By great good fortune, one of the gentlemen I called on proved to be the ideal prospect. He was one of the largest traders, that is, short-term owners of securities, in the state. He was in the process of selling his business to devote full time to this avocation, and he probably had more friends in the city of Baltimore than most politicians did. Looking back, I don't know whether he was impressed by my energy or merely felt sorry for me. In any event, he began to visit me in my office. Although we did no business, I was encouraged to feel that eventually we would.

Within six months I received a telephone call requesting me to meet him in a nearby suburb after the close of the market. When I asked the purpose of the visit, he said he wanted me to meet the managing partner of another firm, with the idea of perhaps joining it. Since my business was just beginning to develop and the other firm was much smaller than the one I was working for, I was naturally reluctant to consider the move. However, this man had been kind to me, so I determined to return the favor. I did meet him that day, and subsequently I was hired by the other firm with a base salary of $8,400 per year. This was a considerable increase, and within 12 months I was well in the $20,000 range. This seemed to me to be a fantastic amount, compared to my previous earnings. In 1960 dollars, it *was* a truly remarkable increase.

The point of this story is that hard prospecting pays off in a number of ways. In my case it gave me a great deal of sales experience compressed into a relatively short period. I forced me to think on my feet and to develop confidence in my own abilities. It brought me, slowly but surely, a growing number of better clients. And, through a stroke of good fortune, it brought me to the attention of the one big trader I needed to be truly successful, since his business and the business of his friends and their subsequent referrals gave me a considerable client base.

As far as I know, very few young account executives in Baltimore have taken to the streets as I did. Later, when I was training young men in the business, I found that they were embarrassed to make cold calls, and many felt that in some way it was demeaning to ask for business. If you are convinced of the value of your product and the value of the services you can perform, you should never be embarrassed about presenting these services to anyone. Whatever financial service you may be selling, nothing will take the place of meeting your prospects face to face.

PROSPECTING FOR CORPORATE SALES

Prospecting for a corporation's business is much different from prospecting for an individual's business. Corporate prospecting is essentially a numbers game in which the salesman who makes the most contacts will generate the most proposals, and the one who makes the most proposals will get the most business. In prospecting individuals, the competition is generally somewhat limited because most of it originates in the immediate geographical area. Also, most competitors are individuals purporting to be salesmen who actually are something much less. In soliciting corporations, particularly the major ones, the competition often comes from national or international companies, and the salesmen are likely to be thoroughly professional in every way.

One offset to the greater competition is the fact that detailed information is much more readily obtainable concerning corporations than it is for individuals. For instance, Dun and Bradstreet publishes annual directories of all corporations with a net worth of $1 million or more and those with a net worth of from $500,000 to $1 million. This firm also makes various information available on cards and tape, so specific groups of prospects can readily be solicited by mail. Standard & Poor's and Moody's both publish daily comprehensive information on publicly owned corporations in this country. Standard and Poor's stock reports are an easy-to-read compilation of information on most of the larger publicly owned companies. Numerous states publish directories containing information on the manufacturers or businesses located in them. In addition, many industries publish directories of various sorts which make it possible to target specific users of a financial service.

To examine the process of prospecting for sales to corporations, we will assume that you are the representative of a regional bank equipment leasing company. Your responsibility is to seek equipment leasing and financing business in a three-state area. Your product is the lease or finance agreement for equipment in the $250,000 to $10 million range.

Step 1

Step 1 is to determine what companies will be your best prospects. To determine this you would first examine the companies' credit. Considering the size transaction you wish to develop, the minimum net worth requirements will probably be $1 million. Larger companies will be better prospects; probably your best prospects will have a net worth of over $2 million. Further, your prospects must be earning in the area of 10 percent after taxes on their net worth to be considered credit worthy. Their earnings record must be reasonably satisfactory for at least the prior three years, and there must be no major problems evident on the horizon.

Your best prospects obviously would be companies that use large amounts of equipment and replace it on a continuing basis. A look through the Dun and Bradstreet directory would indicate that certain SIC or industry classifications are more apt to use your services. Mining companies, some retailers, manufacturers, transportation companies, and utilities tend to use major amounts of equipment. Conversely, furniture stores, financial institutions, architectural firms, engineering firms, most wholesalers, and companies of this type generally use little equipment other than that needed for data processing or office procedures.

Companies' balance sheets also influence their equipment financing. Those with little or no debt are generally not good prospects for equipment leasing or financing, since they have unused borrowing capacity at the banks where they maintain accounts. Companies with major amounts of debt in their capital structure generally find new financing sources worth examining.

You also would investigate the companies' prospects and long-term growth outlook. Companies which are expanding often find their capital requirements are increasing too rapidly to develop sufficient equity. Thus they are excellent prospects for equipment leasing and financing. In contrast, companies whose sales and balance sheets are relatively static usually require little or no outside financing.

At this point, you will have developed a corporate profile that reads as follows: Your best prospect is a company with a net worth in excess of $2 million, earning over $200,000 per year. It has a fair amount of leverage in its capital structure and definite growth plans, and it is in a business where large amounts of equipment are required annually. This profile is simple to determine, but many aspiring salesmen waste time and money every year calling on companies that will never cross the line separating possibles from prospects.

Step 2

The second step is to examine the competition. Assuming you have marked off the market and defined the best prospects, you now must examine their present sources of such funding.

Your most likely competitor will be a prospect's local bank. This is the bank where the company's deposits are maintained and where short-term borrowing can be had at lowest cost, based on the balances normally maintained. Often the local bank will have a member on the board of directors of the company and the firm's president will be on the board of the bank.

The next most common competitor is a regional or major money-center bank. This is the bank that steps in when the local bank is unable to fund a firm's full requirements. It may be working through the local bank or through a loan production office. Sometimes your competitor will be an investment banker which assisted the company in its original formation and has continued to offer advice and arrange public financing. Almost certainly, it would have a member on the board of the company.

Another likely competitor is a major financing company such as General Electric Credit Corporation or Commercial Credit. Competition also comes from other leasing companies; these encompass everything from General Electric Credit Corporation's equipment leasing group to the major money-center banks and local bank lessors. Other competitors are equipment leasing brokers who provide no funds themselves but who represent various financial institutions which do not maintain their own sales forces.

Step 3

In Step 3 you determine as nearly as you can why your prospects are obtaining their equipment leasing and financing from the institutions with whom they are dealing. You will probably find that a number of factors have a bearing on this complex question.

One factor is price—that is, the simple-interest equivalent of the rental figures or financing cost. This factor undoubtedly will have a significant impact on this type of decision. You will find that individual prospects use different methods of evaluating the price of a given financing method. Some will determine the simple-interest rate equivalent of the rentals or look at the total cost of the transaction. Others will determine their time value of money and use it to discount the stream of payments to a present value. It is very important to determine early on which method a prospect is using. This is discussed further in Chapter 6.

The terms of the transaction—that is, the length of the transaction and its special characteristics, such as prepayment penalties, required guarantees, disposition of tax benefits, and the like—will also have an important bearing on a prospect's decision. So will the accounting and tax treatment of the transaction—whether a lease is categorized as "capital" or "operating" for accounting purposes, and whether or not the rental payments are deductible for federal and state income tax purposes.

The prospect's confidence in its prospective sources of funds is frequently overlooked as a reason for doing business with a particular financial institution. Some institutions and individuals have a reputation for performance despite obstacles; others have a reputation for altering or changing transactions after negotiations have substantially been ended. A prospect who had had a bad experience with one lessor will rank the confidence factor very high on his checklist the next time he goes to market.

Many times your prospect will be dealing with an institution because of a long-standing relationship with it which has been mutually satisfactory. Sometimes this source may be more expensive than possible alternatives, but the prospect will continue to do business with it because of the friendship that has developed over a long period.

At various times in the economic and interest cycle, money may be in short supply, and large transactions in the $100 million category always find few takers. In these instances, a prospect may deal with an institution almost solely on the basis of availability. In the first instance, if money is exceptionally tight, old relationships may be broken because a supplier is unable to meet the company's needs. In the second instance, there are only a limited number of institutions that can operate in the $100 million and over area. Therefore, the limited number of players is almost certain to get a certain amount of business regardless of price, terms, confidence, or relationships.

After examining these reasons why your prospects may be dealing with another institution, you must then determine which of these reasons are most likely to cause them to give you at least some of their business. Unless you can develop strength in at least one of these areas, you will find competing most difficult. The more of these factors you can bring to bear on your prospects, the better will be your chance of success.

Step 4

The next step is to determine the advantages of your product. In our example, you must determine why corporations use leasing and/or financing arrangements to secure the use of equipment. The reasons include:

1. Financing or leasing is a generally accepted method of bringing in an entirely new source of funds, beyond normal financing sources. It can be particularly beneficial in the case of a growing company where present sources of funding may already be stretched.

2. Leasing and financing normally entail 100 percent of the cost of the equipment through down payments and other cash distributions. This can be most advantageous for a growing company trying to preserve its working capital.

3. "True" or operating leases provide legitimate off-balance-sheet financing which may be useful to a company that is already highly leveraged.

4. Equipment leasing provides an opportunity for the firm to sell such tax benefits as the investment tax credit and accelerated depreciation, as well as the future residual value of the equipment. As an offset, the lease contains a lower current rate. This can be most important, particularly in such instances as the transportation industries, where large amounts of equipment are acquired annually and profits are often not sufficient to utilize tax benefits fully.

5. Equipment leasing and financing normally allow lessees to avoid most if not all of the negative and positive covenants or agreements contained in other bank or insurance company loans. Avoiding these restrictions may be very valuable from an operational standpoint and well worth any additional costs involved.

6. Companies often use equipment leasing and financing because the amount of money involved, while not large enough for public or private placement, is still so large that taking the money from working capital is not desirable. It may also be too large to fund out of short-term bank loans, which are often viewed as tantamount to working capital.

7. Fixed rates over long terms are often available in equipment leasing and financing, while they might not be available from other sources of funds. The fixing of costs can be very beneficial.

8. A corporation may not wish to assume ownership of some equipment, such as corporate aircraft, in order to avoid possible problems with irate shareholders.

9. Many corporations feel that only assets that appreciate should be owned, whereas assets that depreciate should probably be leased, since their use is more important than their ownership. Such corporations feel that money invested in land and buildings, mineral resources, or timber lands is preferable to investments required to own equipment, the best of which becomes junk at some point in the future.

When prospecting industrial customers, it is necessary to know all of the reasons such prospects might use your product. It is also

Prospecting   63

necessary to be able to explain these reasons in detail and to probe each prospect to see which reasons are appropriate to the specific situation. For instance, if you are calling on a division of General Motors, it is doubtful if providing new sources of funds would be considered a sound reason for using your services. But the ability to provide a GM division with the use of equipment while avoiding ownership might be particularly useful if it were limited as to capital acquisitions. Conversely, if you are calling on a relatively small, fast-growing company, your ability to provide a new source of funds, 100 percent financing, and off-balance-sheet terms, and your offer to trade a lower rate for the firm's tax benefits, which they cannot fully utilize, could very well be overwhelming reasons in your favor.

Step 5

Having determined who your prospects are, who they buy from, why they buy from these institutions, and what their basic reasons are for using the product, you must then determine (as mentioned in Step 3) what specific service or services you can offer to induce them to do business with you and your employer. Since you are the representative of a regional bank equipment leasing company, your price is probably no lower than much of your competition's. You may be able to be somewhat more flexible in constructing transactions so that the terms will be more palatable to your prospect. The types of leases you can offer will probably be those that are standard in the market. As far as availability is concerned, your firm will not be large enough to benefit from the noncompetitive side of the market, but you will have the advantage of availability when some of your competition is out of the market during periods of credit tightness.

If you conduct yourself properly and your firm has a good reputation, you should be able to develop your prospects' confidence, and you may have some relationships already developed which will be useful to you. One thing you will surely be able to offer is service. This means you will offer your ability to assist your prospects in problem solving. Remember, the corporation is not really interested in equipment leasing or financing arrangements per se. What it is interested in is gaining the use of equipment in the most advantageous manner. It is therefore necessary, while prospecting, to probe and probe again to determine what your prospects are actually trying to accomplish. Only then can you assist them to do it successfully.

Step 6

You should now try to determine how to defeat your competition. This is done by accenting your advantages and attempting to solve your prospects' problems in such a manner that the advantages carry enough weight to send the transaction your way. It also entails a system for contacting new prospects and a call-back program for old prospects. Every other week, I require salesmen to place 50 telephone calls a day, which should result in approximately 25 to 30 completed telephone conversations. Personal visits are made on the other weeks, and 12 personal visits a week are considered the minimum. Bear in mind our thesis that in this type of prospecting you are playing a numbers game, and the man who makes the most contacts will probably do the most business.

The requirement to place 250 telephone calls one week and to make at least 12 personal calls the next is considered quite onerous by our salesmen today. As a practical matter, however, all of the men I have trained over the past 17 years have attempted to adhere to this program. It is not a unique idea with me. When I began in the equipment leasing business I worked for Alvin Zises, who insisted that salesmen work one day in the office each week and travel the remaining four days. We were expected to make at least 16 personal calls during the travel period, which required placing close to 50 calls on the one day we were telephoning and using public telephones while traveling to set up the remaining calls.

Zises's basic rules were very simple. They provided that:

1. Salesmen should travel every week and make at least four personal calls every day while traveling.
2. One day a week should be used to set up the next week's travel. In between visits, other telephone calls should be made as follow-up on existing transactions or to set up still further calls. No time should be wasted; a full work day should be allowed every day.

Prospecting 65

3. There are approximately eight hours a day during which a salesman can talk to prospects and customers. Every possible contact should be made during that time, and all other activities, such as letter writing, filing, and traveling, should be done before 9:00 A.M. or after 5:00 P.M. or on weekends.

These salesmen worked harder than any I have seen in the equipment leasing or financing industry. The turnover was substantial, since many could not stand the pace, but those who remained accomplished a great deal. Zises's company developed a portfolio worth hundreds of millions of dollars, although it never employed more than 12 salesmen. Today, many of the "graduates" of this sales school run their own equipment leasing companies or manage the equipment leasing subsidiaries of banks or other financial institutions. The training they received from Alvin Zises undoubtedly provided the equivalent for them of both master's and doctor's degrees in practical business and business product sales.

THE MECHANICS OF PROSPECTING

An inexperienced salesman of big-ticket financial services who is well prepared, psychologically, physically, and mentally, to begin prospecting still may be puzzled about how to proceed. In prospecting for both individual and corporate accounts, interested persons can be contacted with advertising devices such as mass mailings, targeted mailings, newspaper and financial journal advertisements, or television and radio spot commercials. The seminars, courses, and other methods suggested above and other innovative techniques can also be used to build a list of prospects.

At some point, however, it will be necessary to make the initial contact with the prospect, and this is generally done by telephone. The salesman may wonder, "After I dial the prospect's telephone number, what do I actually say?" The purpose of this section is to help you answer that question.

In telephone prospecting, for either individual or corporate sales, you must first assemble all the information required to make your calls. You must have a list of prospects and notes on everything you know about them, and any reference books you might require should be close at hand. The next step is to allot a specific block of time to be devoted solely to prospecting. Attempts to prospect in a sporadic manner have proven ineffective. Your prospects, whether individuals or representatives of corporations, will be most available certain times of the day or night. These are the times you should devote to telephoning.

You should then determine how many calls you plan to complete. If you wish to complete 20 calls, you must be prepared to place about twice that number; it seems almost impossible to reach many people on the first telephone call. Whether calling long distance or locally, you should always give the secretary who will announce your call your name, number, and purpose. No one wants to play guessing games with anonymous callers, and you can expect the people you are calling to be busy and to have even less inclination to do so.

Records should be maintained indicating the number of calls placed and the number completed; the number of prospects who are interested now, who may be interested later, and who are not interested now; and any other pertinent information you can derive from the calls. You should maintain files on all prospects contacted and devise a follow-up system which will ensure future coverage at the times they indicate.

The direct approach is always best, particularly in telephone contacts. After you have reached a prospect, you should come directly to the point, telling him precisely who you are, who you represent, and why you are calling. Aside from being direct, you should also be brief. While the telephone is useful in contacting prospects, it is not the place to give a complete sales talk. Questions that can be answered directly are an effective technique for getting precise information. Examples are: "Are you using my product? If not, why? If so, from whom are you purchasing it? What do you like about their service? What do you dislike about their service? If you have no need for my product now, will you in the future? Why?" It is amazing how willing people are to answer direct, intelligent questions. Within 30 seconds you should have some idea of what your prospect's situation has been, is now, and will be in the future.

This is the time to ask for action—namely, an interview. If it is apparent from the tone of the prospect's voice that there is presently no interest in an interview, you should acknowledge this and ask for a date to be set when an interview would be more appropriate. If an interview is absolutely refused, tell the prospect you are sending a letter and mark the file for recontacting when you think it might be appropriate.

A typical telephone conversation you might have as a salesman prospecting for securities sales would be as follows:

You: Good morning, Mr. Prospect, my name is James Security Salesman. I represent a New York Stock Exchange Company, and I am calling to see if any of our investment services can be useful to you.

Prospect: I'm not interested.

You: Have you ever used the services of a company such as ours?

Prospect: No.

You: Is there any particular reason why you have never used such a firm? Many of them are quite well known, and they advertise nationally. I'm sure you have been contacted by them.

Prospect: I do all of my investing through my bank.

You: Does that save you any money on commissions, Mr. Prospect?

Prospect: No, but I prefer to deal with people I know.

You: I can certainly understand that, Mr. Prospect. At the same time, you had to meet the various people at the bank the first time at some point or another, and you must know of our firm, even though you don't know me. Since you are interested in the type of services we offer, may I suggest that a 15- to 30-minute interview might give us some common ground and be useful to both of us. If it isn't, you at least will have the satisfaction of knowing you are up to date on what is being offered in the market.

At this point the prospect will either cut you off or agree to an interview. If the prospect agrees to the interview, you have had a successful prospecting call. If the prospect refuses the interview, you must probe further to find out why. Bear in mind that you are not attempting to sell the services of your brokerage firm; you are only attempting to sell the interview. I find that the suggestion "What do you have to lose?" often tips the scale in my favor, although I have often received the reply, "15 minutes to one-half hour of my time." My answer to that is that I am also risking my own time, and, furthermore, I will buy the coffee.

No one approach is going to be successful with all prospects. One thing that makes prospecting so interesting is that it presents a series of challenges to your ability to think quickly. There is no easy way to convince every prospect to grant you an interview.

When you are starting out as a salesman of big-ticket financial services it can be very beneficial to work with either a co-worker or a friend acting as the prospect, with the understanding that he or she will be as difficult as possible. Dealing with a difficult person greatly enhances your ability to deal with more routine, politer prospects. This is another facet of the "train hard, fight easy" maxim.

6 | The interview

Setting up and conducting interviews is one of the more pleasant aspects of selling. The method of prospecting suggested in the preceding chapter not only qualifies prospects but also sets up interviews, using the same telephone call to perform both functions. Once possibles have been qualified as live prospects, the next step is the first face-to-face selling effort. This is almost always accomplished with an introductory interview.

INTERVIEWING BASICS: GETTING PAID FOR A BLIND DATE

As in many aspects of selling, the preparation for this interview has a great deal to do with its success. There are certain basic procedures to be followed in setting it up.

Be sure to obtain detailed directions on where the interview is to take place, the best way to reach the location, and, if you will be traveling by car, where to park. If the prospect is located in a large office building, find out the floor on which the individual you are to meet is located, and determine whether you are to go directly to the prospect's office or first to a reception area, perhaps on another floor. If the prospect is located in one of many buildings in an office complex, get explicit directions as to which building it is and how to identify it. You can save yourself a great deal of time and last-minute confusion if you know precisely where the interviewee is located and where you are to report. I have accompanied many salesmen on interviews, and I am constantly amazed at how often they do not know where they are going.

Because in some areas there are streets or roads that have quite similar names but are widely separated, learning the name of an adjacent cross street can be useful. This also helps in areas where adjacent communities share a road or avenue. On such streets the numbering of addresses may go up and down several times in just a few miles, and you can go from community to community without realizing it. I remember spending almost an hour on the Camino Real going down the peninsula from San Francisco because I was not aware that it ran from just outside San Jose to just outside San Francisco, a distance of almost 50 miles, and I failed to realize that every community had its own numbering system.

Most salesmen attempt to be prompt, but you should do better than that and always be at least 15 minutes early for every appointment. This gives you an opportunity to look around and perhaps learn something about your prospect. If you are calling on a corporation officer you can ask for the company's latest report, and if you are calling on an individual investor you can sometimes glean additional information from a receptionist or secretary. The extra 15 minutes also allows the margin you need in case of sudden cancellations so you can fill in with visits to other prospects or find an alternative party with whom you can meet. Inevitably, some prospects will be forced by unforeseen circumstances to cancel their appointments. The waiting time also can be used to scan your interview plan.

The interview plan, a brief written outline of the salient points you intend to make and the more important questions you wish to ask, must be prepared in advance. You should jot down any factual information you have on the individual or corporation, summarizing what you know of the prospect—and you should know as much as possible. In your briefcase you should carry a large lined pad, whatever rate books you may require, and a small calculator, if necessary. You should also carry any printed materials necessary to prove your points or to supply information you may wish to convey. It should be unnecessary to add that you should also have a pen and plenty of business cards, but many salesmen show up at interviews without either.

When you actually meet those you have come to visit, you will find that many of them are more nervous and ill at ease than you are. Often prospects are bracing themselves to say no to any sales talk. They may be ready to take the offensive in order to defend themselves or be basically uncertain about the course of action they ought to take.

In any case, a slightly self-deprecating approach coupled with subtle image building and common sense appear to be most effective. This is the approach I take in meeting new prospects. I shake hands, as customary, and I usually sit down, whether invited to or not.

If I am calling on an individual prospect for a product such as investments, after some brief opening comments I might begin with an observation like, "In this confusing world, brokers are sometimes as confused as anyone else." I would say that my firm has had an exceptional record in working with municipal bonds, or tax shelters, or growth stocks, or whatever our strength might be. Then I would add something like, "You should realize that you are relying not only on my acumen but on the combined resources of my very powerful and prestigious firm."

If I am calling on a corporate prospect for such services as investment banking, I might say something to this effect: "Our firm certainly doesn't have all the answers and, in any event, we don't know enough about your company to make any comments at all now. However, we have had some notable successes." I would then name those successes.

In both cases you will note that I am attempting to impress the prospect that I don't think I have all the answers, but I do have an open mind. I and my company have been generally successful with others, and we will attempt to provide this prospect with the same type of services.

When a prospect mentions a past failing either I or the company was responsible for, I do not attempt to dodge the issue, preferring to meet it head on. I might say something like, "Yes, we failed to call the downturn on the market in 1974. We missed it entirely. But we were not alone, and we *did* catch the upswing in 1975, so we probably came out better than many others who missed both moves in the market." To a corporate prospect who starts the conversation by stating that "equipment leasing is always more expensive than borrowing," I might say, "You're certainly right, at least part of the time, but at other times leasing may actually be less expensive. Certainly, even if it is more expensive, it's worth the extra cost." I would then proceed to tell the prospect *why* it is worth the cost.

In conducting the interview, relax and try to converse with a new client just as you would with an old friend. Being relaxed (as noted in Chapter 2) means sitting comfortably but not sprawling. It means looking prospects in the eye during the conversation, but not to the point where it appears that you're trying to drill holes in them. Direct eye contact is best used for emphasis; you need not hesitate to let your eyes wander if you are reflecting, trying to recall specific information, and the like. During much of a face-to-face conversation you probably will be looking at the prospect somewhere between the nose and the mouth.

A certain amount of opening small talk is not out of place, but you should get to the point quickly. Your interview plan should include a list of prepared questions you wish to ask prospects in order to determine what their needs may be, how they perceive these needs, and how you can possibly meet their requirements.

An essential part of every interview is a call for action, initiated by either yourself or the prospect. In some interviews you will be fortunate enough to close the sale the first time. In many cases, however, success will come only as a result of a long succession of discussions, proposals, and solicitations. No matter how discouraging an interview has been, you should call for some action by either yourself or the prospect. You may offer to send the prospect additional information, such as a written proposal, or you may request the prospect to supply you with missing information. Be sure that someone is definitely going to do something at some predetermined time.

The interview should not be closed without determining a precise follow-up date. Regardless of how encouraging an interview has been, a follow-up date, no matter how remote, should be proposed. If nothing else, this allows you to return to the prospect after whatever period you have specified.

It is impossible to advise you how to handle every interview situation, since they are so varied. After some 30 years in various types of financial sales, I am still occasionally amazed by the twists an interview will take. The accompanying checklist has been prepared as a device you can use after each interview to evaluate its effectiveness and suggest ways to improve your skills as you conduct other interviews.

INTERVIEW CHECKLIST

The following yes-or-no questions should give you an insight into how effective each prospecting interview has been. The number in parentheses indicates the score for each yes answer.

1. Did I see the right person? (30)
2. If I did not see the right person, did I find out who I should have seen? (10)
3. If the answer to 2 is yes, did I arrange to contact the correct person? (10)
4. If the answer to question 2 is no, will I arrange to contact the person very shortly? (10)
5. Did I successfully sell my firm, my product, and myself? (10)
6. Did I discover my prospect's problems and analyze them? Did I understand the prospect's situation? (20)
7. Does the prospect understand my product? (20)
8. Did I make a call for action? (20)
9. Do I have a follow-up date? (20)
10. Did I make the sale? (10)
11. Did I lay the groundwork for future sales? (20)

Total your score and rate yourself as follows:

150 and above	Either you've learned a lot or you didn't need this book! 200 is a perfect score.
120–140	You're doing extremely well. You must become a success.

90–110	You're doing well and should do even better with more work.
60–80	Evidently this was a frustrating interview. You had better give it some real thought. Where did you go wrong? This is not a hopeless situation, but you must do better.
30–50	This is very poor; you need to work on improving most facets of your interview technique. You should try to have an associate accompany you and analyze where you are going wrong.
20 and below	Unless you are joking, you are in deep trouble. Your only hope is to go back to basics. For openers, reread the first six chapters of this book and arrange to have an associate accompany you on every interview until you see substantial improvement. If you really want to succeed you have a chance, but you are hanging by a thread. Unless improvement comes fairly quickly, reading beyond Chapter 6 will not help.

PROBLEMS ENCOUNTERED IN INTERVIEWS
Welcoming objections

More pure nonsense may have been written on the subject of meeting objections than any other topic, except possibly religion and politics. In selling, the object is not to *meet* objections but to *welcome* them. If in an interview you have ever sat face to face with a man and seen his eyelids gradually droop as he fights sleep, or if you have ever watched a woman glance, not too surreptitiously, at her watch about five times a minute, you will realize the worth of objections.

Probably the worst kinds of prospects are those who just won't talk. These are the types that send salesmen in search of liquid solace at the end of the day. Prospects who make objections are at least interested. They have considered their situations and your suggestions, and they are thinking. You are never going to do any business with a prospect who falls off to sleep, or rushes from the

The interview 75

room and never reappears, or leaps from the window, or throws you out of the office. But as long as a prospect continues to think and shows it by listening or at least talking, you still have a chance.

One of the best ways to handle objections is the "yes but" technique. In selling financial services I have often been tempted to let prospects know precisely what I think of their intellectual capabilities, their future and the future of their companies, and their ancestry, and to make various other pertinent and impertinent observations. I have only rarely yielded to this temptation, since in doing so I would obtain satisfaction but very little business. No matter how asinine the objections, it is better to repeat them and then lead in with some comment like "You have an excellent point, but . . ." or "I think I understand your point of view, but . . ." or "Do I understand that it is your position that . . . ?" This allows the prospect to save face and is much more effective than "Listen, jackass, you don't know what you're talking about and you probably never did," no matter how accurate such a statement might be.

The way to hold your temper in such situations is by analyzing the prospects. Look on them as you would some heathen who worships a rock and insists on bashing his toes with it as his method of worship. You would not lose your temper with such an individual but would treat him with patience and consideration, no matter how appalled you were as he smashed his toes one by one with his rock. A prospect, whether an individual or a corporation, who has not had the benefit of your services certainly deserves the same consideration.

You may think I am treating a serious subject with undue levity. But if you, like I, had listened to a few thousand people who didn't really know what they were talking about express their views in very definite and often strident terms, you would realize that a sense of humor is exactly what is required in meeting objections. It doesn't pay to get angry, it doesn't pay to get tense. You have to play the game of "I won't fight."

Uncovering hidden objections

One of the most important points in what I consider to be the greatest book on sales every written, *How I Raised Myself from Failure to Success in Selling*, is that prospects, whether individual or corporate, will often reject a sale on the basis of some hidden objection.* They may not discuss it or even know (on a conscious level) that it exists. A man asked to purchase life insurance for the protection of his wife and five children, for example, says, "I don't have enough money," when he means, "I don't want to think about death." A corporate treasurer says, "We don't believe in equipment leasing," when she means "We are forbidden under our borrowing agreements from using any other financing." The president of a company says, "We always deal with the same New York investment banker and do not want to make a change," when he means, "My brother-in-law works for that broker and I *can't* change."

There is no simple way to find the hidden objection. You must keep probing until the prospect's answers make sense. I have found that if prospects will continue to answer questions, I can usually determine precisely why they are not using my services. It is only when they stop talking that I hit a brick wall and have to start guessing.

Generally, hidden objections are based on the fear of something happening if the decision to use a financial service is made. An individual purchasing financial services may fear a loss, and a corporation may fear a loss or an adverse accounting treatment or other organizational consequence.

A hidden objection may also be based on embarrassment. An individual may be embarrassed to say that he can't afford your services, or he has made commitments elsewhere, or he doesn't understand what you are attempting to do for him. In the case of a corporation, the embarrassment may be due to severe restrictions placed on the corporation by various borrowing agreements, or a contact may be embarrassed because she doesn't have the authority she feels she should have.

Uncertainty is another common cause of hidden objections. An individual may be uncertain as to the benefits or costs of the services you are selling, or unsure of personal long-range goals. In a corporate situation, the corporation's planning may be weak and its needs uncertain, or your contacts may be uncertain as to the value of your services or their ability to understand them.

---

* Frank Bettger, *How I Raised Myself from Failure to Success in Selling* (Englewood Cliffs, N.J.: Prentice-Hall, 1958).

Usually, if the hidden objection can be found, it can be surmounted. Often you will find that your possibilities of obtaining the business have been enhanced because your competitors have merely accepted an apparent objection and have never uncovered the hidden objection underlying it. Thus they never come close to winning the business.

In addition to the sense of humor needed in coping with any objection, uncovering a hidden objection also requires a great deal of patience to probe, question, placate, and soothe a prospect and eventually find the real problem.

Converting to dollars and cents

Another interview technique that is helpful in selling a financial service to either individuals or corporations is to show the prospect how the problem and the cost of the service can be converted to dollars and cents. For example, in attempting to sell investment services to an individual, it is helpful to express the situation in quantitative terms, as in the following statement:

> Mr. Prospect, we are suggesting that you invest $100,000, which will return you $7,000 per year in dividends and give you a potential long-term capital gain of $50,000 over the next five years. The cost of our services is something like a thousand dollars in brokerage fees. Even without the capital gains, if your investment merely stays as it is, with no appreciation, your net return will be $6,000 the first year and $7,000 thereafter, with an excellent possibility of increasing those amounts as the dividends increase. If you were to purchase real estate at the same cost, the commission would be $7,000 to $8,000, and you would be fortunate, in today's market, to realize the same cash flow. You also would not have as liquid an investment. The investment we suggest can be turned into cash, *entirely or in part,* within a week.

Likewise, in attempting to sell equipment leasing services to a corporation, for example, you could point out that the aftertax cost of obtaining $1 million at a fixed rate is only 3 or 4 percent, while the equipment is expected to produce aftertax profits of almost 20 percent. Obviously, this is a very satisfactory projection for the corporation.

If the dollars and cents prove to be detrimental to your sales pitch, you are in the wrong business. What you are selling must make sense to your prospects from a dollars-and-cents standpoint. If you are to be successful on a continuing basis, your product, no matter what it is, must deliver value. If it doesn't, any success you may enjoy will be of very brief duration.

When you meet a good salesman on a social basis, notice that he doesn't attempt to sell you his product then, but he does let you know that his company is one of the tops in the field, that its product is excellent, and that he is one of the more successful purveyors of it. In every contact you make with a prospect, particularly in the interview, you must attempt to present such an image for your company, your product, and yourself. Even though you may be new to selling your product, you can be knowledgable about it, and you can sell yourself as well as your company and its product.

Finding the decision maker

One of the more difficult situations you can encounter in an interview is to realize that the party with whom you are talking is not the decision maker and will not attempt to influence the decision maker as you wish. The way to head off this situation, of course, is to prevent it by making sure that you are calling on the proper person to begin with. Once you have gotten off to a bad start, however, your only recourse is to make the best of it. If you are calling on the wrong individual, say the son when you should be talking to the father, or the husband when you should be talking to the wife, the situation is fairly easy to deal with. You can say you have enjoyed chatting with the person and now will contact the other family member because you are confident they also will be interested in hearing what you have to say. Note that you don't ask for permission to talk to anyone. If the permission should be denied, you would be placed in direct conflict with your prospect should you decide to follow your own best interests.

In the corporate environment this is a more difficult situation. Because decision makers usually make it a policy to back their subordinates, if your approach blatantly rejects a subordinate you are not going to make very good progress. The subordinate's prestige is very much at stake, and there probably is no better way to make an enemy than to show contempt for a subordinate by going over his head. In this situation, the best approach is to appeal to the subordinate, somewhat as follows:

> Mr. Prospect, I feel that you have given me a very fair hearing but, despite my best efforts, I have not been able to convince you. My employer will tolerate my losing business, but he won't tolerate my failure to try every avenue to attain success. For that reason, I would like your cooperation in contacting your superior to tell my story there.

Note that again you do not ask for permission. You ask for cooperation and give a very plausible reason why it is important to you. Furthermore, while you may somewhat overstate the case, you are essentially telling the truth, because no employer will tolerate a salesman who doesn't try everything to succeed, nor should you be satisfied with anything less than an all-out effort. If the subordinate will introduce you to the superior, you can obtain the latter's full attention and avoid any semblance of conflict.

This approach does not always work, but I think it is the best way to handle a very difficult situation. A variant of this situation which is always easier to handle occurs when your contact is not the decision maker and has very little real input or interest in the decision. Chances are the party you should be seeing is operating on about the same level in some other group or division of the corporation. In this case, it is much easier to get your contact, who has little or no interest, one way or another, in the outcome, to put you in touch with the person you should talk to. You will find that the difference between a seasoned, professional salesman and a novice is that the former will ask for and obtain an introduction to the proper party, whereas the latter will often spend a great deal of time with the wrong person.

It is never wise to go around original contacts when you know they will be offended unless you can prove that the corporation employing them will suffer a major loss unless you do. The operative words here are *prove* and *major loss*. If you *think* the firm could suffer a loss but you are not sure it would be a major one, or if a major loss could occur but you are not able to prove that it *will* occur if your advice is not taken, you are on very shaky ground. In my own experience, in the few instances I have made a point to go over a subordinate's head I have failed to sell my product. Further, I have had very little likelihood of ever doing any business with these firms as long as the original cast of characters is still in place. I may have obtained some personal satisfaction, but the financial results were nil.

Sometimes the interview must be used to find the right individual to contact in a major corporation. When you determine that your original contact is not the person you should be seeing, the best way to find the right one without offending anyone is to explain in detail what your objectives are. Then ask your contacts to define their functions and designate the persons with whom they interface. Drawing an organizational chart for the prospect's company can be very useful in establishing whom you should be seeing. You may find that you should be calling on a number of people if the corporation is large enough.

The important thing is to ask questions when you need to know more about prospects. It is also important to make sure that both you and the persons you are visiting are using the same terms to mean the same things. People who spend a great deal of time in an industry or profession often develop their own jargon, and when they are dealing with the general public, they may find the terms are not understood.

I vividly recall calling on the chief financial officer of a major airline with one of our salesmen in an attempt to sell equipment leasing. During the interview, which lasted well over an hour and was very congenial, the financial officer assured us a number of times that the airline was doing no leasing. Toward the end of the interview, just as we were getting ready to leave, the salesman asked the question we should have asked at the outset: "How *do* you finance your aircraft?" The reply was that they were being financed under conditional sales agreements. Now, to a leasing salesman, any type of equipment contract which provides for the use of the equipment can be categorized as a lease, whether or not it really is one from a tax and legal viewpoint. In this case, the prospect was using the term *lease* in a narrow but correct connotation, and we were using it in an imprecise but generally accepted manner. Not until we both defined our terms did our visit become meaningful. Afterward, the salesman and I wondered how many opportunities we had lost because we did not fully understand what the prospect was telling us, or the prospect did not fully understand what we were saying.

7 | Issuing proposals

The most usual way to follow up on the call for action with which every effective interview ends is with a proposal offering the prospect specific services. Issuing a proposal provides the final opportunity in prospecting to find out precisely what your prospective client wants and to offer just that.

The purpose of this book is to help you become a top professional salesman of big-ticket financial services, not to provide detailed technical information. But a proposal is potentially a legal document, and before you can issue one for the prospect's possible acceptance, you must have some familiarity with the various laws affecting contracts and frauds. If your education or experience has not supplied this information, or your present employer has offered no help, you should make it a point to familiarize yourself with the laws in your jurisdiction.

LEGAL COMPLEXITIES

This chapter will give you enough background information so you will at least be aware of the complexities of the laws affecting a salesman's offers of financial services. In addition, the American Institute of Banking has allowed me to excerpt extensively from its fine book *Law and Banking*, and the second half of this chapter consists of sections taken from this work.

The law of contracts

My pocket dictionary defines the word *contract* as a "legal agreement." It defines the word *offer* as "to tender or proffer," *proffer* meaning to propose or to bid. The dictionary also defines the word *acceptance* as "an accepting or reception taken willingly" or "agreement to."

These uncomplicated definitions may make you think that the law of contracts is a simple one. This would be a serious mistake. Depending on the jurisdiction, it is a labyrinth, as complicated as anything you could possibly imagine. Its nuances are numerous and delicate, and even experienced practicing attorneys sometimes find it unfathomable.

In layman's terms, a contract is a legal binding promise. It applies when one party makes an offer to do something or perform some service, based on certain circumstances, and the other party accepts the transaction as offered. Basic to contract law is the concept that there must be a consideration; that is, the offeror who tenders something of value must receive something of value in return from the offeree. Further, the contract is void if its purpose is illegal.

As a general rule, until there is acceptance, the offeror is free to revoke the offer, at which time the offeree may no longer make acceptance. To complicate things further, the offeree may accept but under changed circumstances, in which case the original offeror may in certain cases be considered to have accepted the changed acceptance, even though that may not have been the intention.

There is a popular misconception that a contract must be in writing to be valid. This is, of course, not correct. If oral contracts do not violate the statute of frauds, which provides that certain types of promises are enforceable only if they are in writing and signed, they can be completely binding. The problem is to prove that an oral contract exists, and this can be quite difficult. Proving its terms and conditions may be almost impossible.

The public customarily categorizes the financial community as expressing its terms in "weasel wording." The verbal hedging in most documents relating to proposals, however, is used specifically to avoid potential problems that might be encountered under contract law. If you are selling equipment financing, for example, you must be very careful to note that a proposal issued to a prospective client is tentative in nature, and you must specify all the circumstances to be met before it can be accepted. Otherwise the prospect may accept the proposal as written, and you may find yourself forced into unwillingly performing as proposed, or else fighting a lawsuit.

Any proposals sent to clients should be thoroughly, critically examined by counsel before they are issued, and a salesman should never alter the format on his own initiative. All offers, regardless of the type of service proposed, should be hedged by informing prospects that they are contingent upon approval by the salesman's superiors, or subject to legal review, or are in some way not *firm* offers. Habitually expressing your intentions in this way will help you avoid many problems. It is also wise to document any conversations which might be useful in later evaluation of whether a firm or a conditional offer has been made. Your best defense against potential problems is to get into the habit of hedging every statement.

An example of the problems you can encounter in issuing proposals is a situation in which I found myself embroiled some time ago. I issued a tentative proposal to a major corporation, contingent upon the corporation doing three things. The corporation accepted my proposal as written, but a month and a half later it indicated that it wished to change the first condition. While, it said, it could not do precisely what it had agreed to, it would do something "as good as." My firm did not agree to waive its prior conditions, but I did agree to examine the suggested alternative, the development of which took a number of months. Finally, our counsel came up with a way the corporation could accomplish what it was attempting to do. Neither I nor any member of management of my company agreed to this alternative, however. As a matter of fact, we determined that the alternative fell far short of being "as good as" what I had originally proposed.

Meanwhile, one of my contacts had maneuvered himself into a very bad position with his employer, since, if this funding did not go through, it would leave a serious gap in the corporation's plans. Therefore he informed his superiors that we had accepted the revised proposal. We, of course, denied it. They engaged an attorney and threatened to bring suit. We engaged an attorney who denied they had grounds for a suit. The threat of a suit was later dropped, but only after my firm had wasted almost a year of management's time and had run up a legal bill of over one quarter of a million dollars.

To avoid these consequences we should not have assumed without question we were dealing with well-disposed, knowledgeable businessmen. We should have documented every phase of the corporation's revised acceptance and continually put it in writing that the suggested alternatives were not acceptable to us. Our failure to dot every *i* and cross every *t* cost us a great deal of money.

Laws concerning fraud

The law concerning frauds also affects proposals offering services to prospects. Even though you and your company are completely legitimate, you may at some point become overly optimistic about the advantages of your product or its possible effects upon its user. If you cross the line between harmless puffery and outright deception, you are guilty of fraud.

Salesmen of big-ticket financial services customarily deal in dollar amounts which make it profitable for anyone who feels aggrieved to bring suit against them and their firms. It is essential, therefore, for the salesman to be very candid and very honest in evaluating the services he is offering.

If you are selling services to individuals, I believe it would be insane to guarantee investment results or anything of the sort that depends on changing market conditions. If you are dealing in the corporate area, it would be very foolish to guarantee that your product is less expensive than any other, since you can't possibly know the cost of all of the other products being offered. In both types of sales, it would be inadvisable to give legal or financial advice without hedging and limiting your accountability.

The following true story illustrates how even an innocent bystander can find himself in trouble, accused of misrepresentation. Some years ago I was in the securities business as a registered representative or salesman for a major New York Stock Exchange firm. All the salesmen sat at desks in a common room, and each desk had a visitor's chair. It was customary for clients to visit the salesmen, although any real privacy was impossible.

At the time of this incident the local partner and the sales manager were deeply interested in the stock of a local company, and they were urging all their clients to purchase it. I did not feel that this security was suitable for most of my clients because it was a new company and its future was uncertain. While there was the possibility of tremendous gains, there was also the possibility of complete loss, since the company might not survive.

The salesman who sat in front of me liked to say, as a joke, "This stock will send me to Florida." He would add that if the company prospered, he could afford to go to Florida to live, and if it didn't he would have to leave town, and Florida would be his probable destination. As part of his sales pitch, he often used the phrase, "This stock will send your children to college."

One day my largest customer, an in-and-out trader who bought and sold mostly New York Stock Exchange stocks for a quick turnaround, overheard this salesman giving his pitch. He asked me what I thought of the company, and I told him what I have told you. I also told him that it really was not his kind of stock, since it was traded over the counter, and it required a long-term investor. Unfortunately, I was not able to dissuade him, and he bought 100 shares at about $132 per share, which later proved to be very close to the all-time high for this stock. Some six months later the local company was virtually out of business, and the stock, which had split 3 for 1, was being traded at the equivalent of about $15, a considerable drop from its high of $135.

About a year later, this customer became part of a class action suit brought against the broker and myself. I was called to make a deposition, and the attorney for my former client (by this time, he was a *former* client) asked me, "Did you tell Mr. X that this security would send his children to college?" I replied by asking the attorney how well he knew Mr. X, and the look on his face showed that he did not know his client very well. I told him that Mr. X was about 60 years old and that his youngest child at the time he bought the security was a senior in college. Further, his wife was ill and had been in a sanitorium for years, and it was unlikely he would have younger children to be "put through college" by this security. Anyone who knew Mr. X would not have used that phrase to sell him a security or anything else, so it was obvious that I had not said what Mr. X claimed I had. In fact, I had not made any statements of a similar nature, and I was able to produce witnesses who testified to my attempts to discourage the purchase.

With the passage of time, I have become convinced that Mr. X was so busy listening to the salesman who sat in front of me and so swayed by his sales story that he actually did think I had said this stock would put his children through college, however illogical that would have been. Certainly the other salesman had gone far beyond acceptable puffery, and, although his joking was well meant, in my opinion he had been guilty of fraud. I was released from any liability, but I understand the brokerage firm did make a considerable settlement with all of the buyers of that security who made claims.

PROCEDURES AND SAFEGUARDS

Experiences such as this emphasize the need to keep to the point and to be completely honest in issuing proposals. Every proposal should be prepared so that it meets the standards of fairness, completeness, and specificity, and its appearance should be appropriate to the subject and the recipient. All the pertinent facts and conditions should be included, and costs should be expressed as clearly as possible, in percentages and actual dollars if practical. The proposal also should have an expiration date.

Two general methods are used in issuing proposals: bids and negotiations. The bid method can operate very much in the used-car sales mold. The standard approach is the "low ball": unrealistically low-cost proposals are issued, with the idea of winning the transaction by offering the lowest bid and then persuading the prospect to accept less advantageous terms. As far as I am concerned, this method is not only unethical, it is possibly illegal, and it certainly is unproductive over the long term. Any salesman who wishes to make a name for himself and his company in the money business will find that it is truly destructive to build a reputation for unreliability. Furthermore, this approach encourages prospects in constant efforts to renegotiate a transaction.

A better approach is to always come in with your best numbers and then be willing to negotiate the terms. Price should be held inviolable, however. As a matter of general practice, it is much more desirable to negotiate a transaction than to bid against numerous competitors on the basis of price alone, since price may be but a small part of the transaction. In my view, the best approach is to sell a negotiated transaction based on offers of superior service.

Geographical and time limitations may make it necessary to mail some proposals, but it is preferable to hand deliver a proposal and to sit down with the prospect and go over it line by line. Often the prospect will not understand what might appear to you to be a simple proposal.

Some time ago I issued a proposal to lease various equipment to a midwestern utility, quoting a quarterly factor of 3.9728 percent of cost. The proposal explained that the quarterly rental for any amount of money was obtained by multiplying the figure by this factor. When I phoned my contact to go over the proposal, I was told that the annual rate (which was actually 3 percent simple interest) was much too high, since 4 times 3.9728 percent was 15.8912 percent, and at that time this utility could obviously obtain money at considerably lower cost. It took a great deal of explaining to get through to this individual that the factor included both amortization of the principal and interest, and it was in fact equivalent to a much lower simple interest rate. As I hung up the phone, I thought how incredible it was that a supposed financial expert did not realize what a quarterly payment factor really meant. I wondered how many transactions I had won or lost because the pospect did not understand what I, or perhaps my competitor, was proposing.

This experience points up the advisability of explaining every facet of a proposal in detail. Doing this in person also supplies an occasion to see competitors' proposals, which of course cannot be done over the telephone. If a prospect is hesitant to show you a competitor's proposal, explain that you would have no objections if your proposal were shown to a competitor. The more you know about your competition and what it is proposing, the better equipped you will be to handle a transaction. While cutting rates to meet or beat the competition is not advisable, renegotiating terms always is. If prospects want a different product or the same product packaged differently, you can only profit by trying to accommodate them.

EXTRACTS FROM *LAW AND BANKING**

1. When do promises become legally, and not merely morally, enforceable? Can these questions be answered by reference to the formal definitions of the terms "promise," "moral commitment," and "contract"?

A "promise" is an undertaking, expressed by words or by conduct, that something will happen or will not happen in the future. The one making the promise (the promisor) undertakes a present commitment of future performance. If the duty that arises as a result of this undertaking is one that the law will enforce, there is said to be a contract between the promisor and the promisee (the recipient of the promise). If the duty does not create legally enforceable rights, it is said to be merely moral, and no contract exists.

It should be clear that the definitions of the words "promise," "moral commitment," and "contract" cannot of themselves resolve the basic question as to which promises the law will enforce, because common definitions of these terms tend to beg that question by defining "contracts" as enforceable promises and "moral commitments" as unenforceable promises.

The basic question of which promises the law will enforce can be answered, however, by looking at the promises that the courts have enforced and gleaning from them the essential elements of contracts.

2. Case law makes it clear that a contract comes into existence when four requisites are satisfied: (1) legal capacity; (2) legal objective; (3) mutual assent; (4) consideration.

3. If the object of the contract is illegal, at least one of the parties, if not both, can avoid the obligation by pleading the illegality. Thus it is said that the objective must be legal before an agreement becomes legally enforceable.

It would be difficult to list all the kinds of illegal agreements, but in general it may be said that the most common types are: (1) agreements

---

* The following sections are reproduced from the American Institute of Banking publication *Law and Banking*. Copyright © 1971, American Bankers Association. Reprinted with permission. All rights reserved.

in restraint of trade; (2) agreements harmful to the public interest; (3) agreements harmful to the marriage relationship; (4) agreements to injure third parties; (5) agreements calling for excessive interest; (6) wagering agreements; and (7) other agreements that violate the positive criminal law.

4. A contract does not come into being until the parties agree to the same bargain at the same time. The concurrence as to terms and time is sometimes said to be a "meeting of the minds." Stated differently, many courts have said that no contract comes into being until there is a meeting of the minds. These decisions, however, oversimplify the problem, because there is yet no way to determine what a man is thinking. To make the law of contracts predictable and capable of administration, the courts universally hold that a man's actual thoughts are irrelevant, and it is only his objectively manifested intention that counts. In other words, it is correct to say that a contract requires a meeting of the minds if presence or absence of this concurrence is determined solely by what the parties communicate to one another, rather than by what their subjective thoughts might have been. This idea was expressed in the leading English case of *Smith* v. *Hughes* by Lord Blackburn in the following manner:

> If, whatever a man's real intention may be, he so conducts himself that a reasonable man would believe that he was assenting to the terms proposed by the other party, and that other party upon that belief enters into the contract with him, the man thus conducting himself would be equally bound as if he had intended to agree to the other party's terms.

The Restatement of Contracts states the matter in this way:

> Mutual assent to the formation of informal contracts is operative only to the extent that its is manifested. Moreover, if the manisfestation is at variance with the mental intent ... it is the expression which is controlling. Not mutual assent but a manifestation indicating such assent is what the law requires.

Not only must the mutual assent be objectively manifested, it also must be communicated to the other in most cases. It is not enough for a party to manifest in some way that he is willing to enter into a contract on the terms proposed to him by another unless he communicates this willingness to the other. Usually, of course, the objective manifestation of mutual assent is found in the communications, but theoretically there is a difference between the two.

Usually the manifestation of mutual assent arises through the process of an offer by one party and an acceptance by the other. According to the Restatement of Contracts:

> This rule is rather one of necessity than of law. In the nature of the case one party must ordinarily first announce what he will do before there can be any manifestation of mutual assent. It is theoretically possible for a third person to state a suggested contract to the parties and for them to say simultaneously that they assent to the suggested bargain, but such a case is so rare and the decision of it is so clear that it is practically negligible.

In discussing the concept of mutual assent, therefore, lawyers usually think in terms of offer and acceptance.

5. An offer is a promise conditioned upon a thing to be done by the offeree. The condition may be the performance of an act, in which case the offer is said to be "unilateral," or it may be the giving of a promise, in which case the offer is said to be "bilateral." The effect of the offer is to confer upon the offeree a legal power to turn the offeror's conditional promise into an absolute one by satisfying the terms of the condition. The acceptance occurs when the offeree satisfies all the conditions of the offer. Until there is an acceptance, as a general rule, the offeror is free to revoke his offer and destroy the power of the offeree to make the offeror's promise absolute. The offeree also can destroy his own power of acceptance by rejecting the offer. These rules and principles are the basic ones of the law of offer and acceptance.

6. Once it is concluded that an offer has been made, it becomes important to determine whether or not it has been accepted and a contract formed. Acceptance occurs when the conditions stated in the offer have been satisfied. The determination of whether or not acceptance has occurred, therefore, is largely the process of ascertaining the existence and scope of the conditions of the offer and deciding whether the offeree has satisfied them. These are matters that are determined by a reasonable interpretation of the offer and a factual ascertainment of what the offeree has or has not done.

Obviously, only the person to whom the offer is addressed may accept it. This proposition is sometimes stated in terms of condition—the condition being that only the person to whom the offer is addressed may accept it.

Since an offer is part of the mechanism of mutual assent, and since mutual assent must be communicated to be legally effective, an offer is

Issuing proposals 91

not effective unless it has been communicated to the offeree. Courts sometimes express this rule in terms of condition—the condition being that the acceptance be made in response to the offer.

The acceptance, of course, must occur within the time limit stated in the offer. If no time limit is stated, the acceptance must be made within a "reasonable time." Circumstances, the usage of the trade, and the special facts of the particular case are relevant in determining whether or not a reasonable time has elapsed.

For purposes of time computations, the acceptance normally is said to be effective and completed as soon as it is dispatched if the means of transmission is one that the offeror has authorized. Customary means of communication, such as letters and telegrams, are authorized for purposes of this rule, unless the offeror specifies to the contrary or the peculiar circumstances of the transaction make it clear that they are not appropriate.

In computing the time period, normally the first day is not counted but all intervening holidays and days are counted, unless the final day falls on a Sunday or holiday, in which case "a day of grace," or additional day, is given.

The acceptance, of course, must comply exactly with the requirements of the offer. A reply to an offer that purports to accept it but that adds qualifications to it is not an acceptance but a rejection and counteroffer.

An acceptance which requests concessions or even a change of terms can still be effective as an acceptance if it really assents to all the conditions of the offer. Lawyers sometimes call this a "grumbling acceptance."

Normally an offer may be revoked at any time before it is accepted. The revocation, however, is not effective as such until it is received by the offeree. A revocation cannot be made after the offer is accepted.

Three exceptions apply to the rule that an offer may be revoked at any time prior to acceptance. The first concerns options. The second concerns offers to enter into unilateral contracts where the offeree has begun the required performance but has not completed it at the time of the purported revocation. The third involves firm offers made in chattel sale transactions.

When a promise to keep an offer open is supported by consideration, an option is created, and it cannot be revoked by the offeror during its stated time period.

Where the offeree of an offer to enter into a unilateral contract has started performance, the offeror loses his power of revocation, but no contract is formed until the offeree performs the act required by the offer.

Under the law of sales of goods, a special rule has developed that is applicable to merchants. If a merchant in a signed writing states that his offer to sell or buy goods will not be revoked, a "firm offer" is created. According to the Uniform Commercial Code, firm offers—even if not supported by consideration—are irrevocable.

In addition to revocation, there are a number of ways in which an offer may be terminated. The most obvious terminating event is a lapse of time or the happening or nonhappening of a condition stated in the offer as causing termination. For example, if the offer were to state that it would expire if the Dow-Jones stock average fell to 900, the occurrence of this event would terminate the offer.

In addition to terminating events stated in the offer itself, the courts have said that an offer is terminated by a rejection of the offeree, by the offeror's death, by an event which deprives the offeror of legal capacity to make a contract, by the death or destruction of a person or thing essential for the performance of the proposed contract, or by the supervening legal prohibition of the proposed contract.

We have seen that a rejection terminates the offer and deprives the offeree of the power of acceptance. This rule cannot be waived by the offeror.

We also have seen that a contract requires two or more persons having legal capacity. The death or legal incapacity of the offeror terminates the offer because it prevents these essential matters from existing. Similarly, the death of the offeree or his loss of legal capacity will terminate the offer if the offer is directed only to him. As we shall see, if it is impossible to perform the contract, the law excuses the performance. As a corollary of this principle, it is said that the death or destruction of a person or thing essential for the performance of the proposed contract terminates the offer. Finally, we have seen that a contract cannot come into being unless its object is a lawful one. From this it follows that the supervening legal prohibition of the proposed contract will automatically terminate the offer.

7. It is not enough to make a contract that the parties, having legal capacity and a legal objective in mind, mutually agree on a set of terms. The contract does not come into existence until these things exist and consideration is given. Therefore, it is correctly said that a legally sufficient and adequate consideration is one of the requirements of a contract.

No legal system in any country has gone so far as to declare that all promises must be performed—even those made by people with legal capacity and with a legal objective in mind who come to full agreement.

It is felt that there should be some freedom to change one's mind with respect to promises made foolishly, or on the spur of the moment through an impulse of generosity, courtesy, or gratitude, to persons who have given nothing in return. Protection is given in Anglo-American law against these follies through the doctrine of consideration. A promise is not enforceable unless consideration has been given for it.

Consideration is the price for the promise. In most cases it is relatively easy to determine whether or not consideration exists, but the definition of the term is somewhat complicated. Consideration is either an act of forbearance or a return promise bargained for and given in exchange for a promise. Textwriters usually define consideration in terms of legal detriment or legal benefit, although courts have emphasized legal detriment in determining whether consideration is present. The promisee sustains legal detriment—and thus gives consideration—when, at the request of the promisor and in reliance on the promise, he does something he was not already legally bound to do, or refrains from doing something he had a legal right to do.

The legal detriment becomes consideration only if it is requested by the promisor. Doing something that may be highly detrimental is not consideration for a promise if the promisor did not request it, for in that case it cannot be argued that it is the price paid for the promise.

As previously noted, textwriters often maintain that consideration can consist of legal benefit to the promisor as well as legal detriment to the promisee, but the courts emphasize detriment, and it is doubtful in most cases that they could be persuaded to find consideration where no legal detriment exists. Consideration must be both adequate and sufficient to make promises binding. Adequacy of consideration means that the detriments incurred on each side of the bargain must be roughly equal. Since the courts are reluctant to police bargains and have no way of determining in most cases whether the prices exchanged by the parties are equal, adequacy or consideration is usually presumed. It is only in those cases in which it is impossible to presume that the exchanges between the two parties are equal that the courts find inadequacy and hence no consideration. This occurs when one of the parties agrees to transfer money or fungible goods (i.e., goods of which any unit is, by nature or usage of trade, the equivalent of any other like unit, as, for example, wheat or oil) as "consideration" for a promise by the other to transfer at the same time and place a larger amount of money or goods of the same kind and quality.

There is sufficiency of consideration when there is a legal detriment on each side of the bargain.

The doctrine of consideration is peculiar to Anglo-American law. It has no place in the laws of France, Italy, Germany, Spain, Holland, Switzerland, Japan, and many other commercial nations. In these countries, a promise is enforceable if it shows on its face the intention to assume a legal obligation. While the experience of these countries has caused some American and English scholars to attack the doctrine of consideration, at the present time the doctrine retains much of its vigor, and there are few exceptions to it. The four principal exceptions which need no consideration to be binding are: (1) promises to pay debts barred by the statute of limitations; (2) promises to pay debts discharged in bankruptcy; (3) promises to perform a voidable duty (under some circumstances); and (4) promises supported by promissory estoppel.

8. Many oral contracts are completely valid. Therefore, it is incorrect to say that a writing is essential to the formation of a contract. There are, however, some contracts that, for reasons of social policy, must be in writing to be enforceable. These contracts are governed by the statute of frauds.

The statute of frauds, so called because it was intended to prevent fraud and perjury in the proving of contracts before the courts, was enacted by the English Parliament in 1677 and has been adopted in whole or in part by all the American states. It provides that certain types of promises are enforceable only if in writing and signed by the person to be charged. The types of promises embraced within the statute of frauds are: (1) promises made in consideration of marriage; (2) promises by executors or administrators to pay a debt of the deceased out of their own pockets; (3) promises which by their terms cannot be performed within one year from the time of the making of the promise; (4) promises to answer for the debt of another; (5) contracts for the sale of land, or any interest in land; and (6) contracts for the sale of goods above the value fixed in the statute.

To this list may be added special statutory rules requiring particular contracts to be in writing. For example, the Uniform Commercial Code requires a writing for contracts involving the sale of securities and the acquisition of security interests in addition to a rule, listed as point (6) above, stating that the sale of goods at a price of $500 or more must be in writing to be enforceable.

The six areas covered by the statute of frauds reflect concern with respect to special situations in which the parties are especially vulnerable to fraud or where the temptation to fabricate may be strong. For example, a disappointed creditor who finds that his debtor has died leaving an insufficient estate to pay his bills may be tempted to claim that the executor or administrator had promised to pay the debt. To protect executors (persons named in a will to settle the estate of a deceased person) and administrators (persons appointed by the court to act if the will names no executor or if there is no will) from this mischief, the statute of frauds provides that any promise by an executor or administrator to "answer damages out of his own estate must be in writing in order to be enforceable."

The interpretation of the statute of frauds by the courts over the years has led to some distinctions not readily found in the statute itself. It is not sufficient, therefore, to simply know the kinds of situations to which the statute of frauds is addressed. It is also necessary to know how the courts have construed its language.

9. After a contract is made, legal attention turns to the matter of performance. As we shall see, the general rule is that the parties must do exactly the things they have promised. While this rule seems obvious, it does have exceptions, and it is complicated by the fact that courts frequently must determine the meaning of words or terms in the contract where the parties have been unclear in their expression. It is one thing to say that the parties must perform all the terms of the contract; it is another thing to determine what those terms are.

"Interpretation" or "construction" is the process of determining the meaning of words or terms of the contract. Although courts resort to common sense in carrying out this process, several primary rules of interpretation have been developed for guidance, and many more "secondary" rules are used when the primary rules do not lead to clear answers.

10. One primary rule of interpretation is called the "parol evidence rule." This rule is sometimes incorrectly stated as one that gives priority to written terms over oral terms. Thus it is sometimes said that oral understandings never can be used to contradict a written contract. But this says too much. The parol evidence rule applies only to oral agreements made prior to or contemporaneously with the formation of a written contract which is intended by the parties to be the complete and final expression of their rights and duties. It does not apply to oral agreements made after the written contract is executed, and it has no application to situations in which the written contract is not intended by the parties to be the complete and final expression of their rights and duties.

The parol evidence rule is also limited in other respects. Fully integrated or merged written contracts, for example, cannot be used to prevent one from establishing fraud based on oral understandings. Additionally, one may establish through parol (oral) evidence that no contract was ever made, even in the face of a written document purporting to be a fully integrated agreement.

11. Another primary rule of interpretation is that words are to be given their plain and usual meaning. Three exceptions to this rule are recognized: (1) usage of the trade or locality may vary the usual meaning of words; (2) technical words ("words of art") are to be given their technical meaning; and (3) words may not be given their plain meaning if that construction contradicts the intention of the parties.

12. The fundamental rule of contract interpretation is that the contract should be construed so as to best effectuate the intention of the parties. As a corollary to this principle, courts sometimes say that they must read the contract as a whole and attempt to give consistent meaning to all the words and terms. This is another way of saying that if the contract contains clauses or terms that appear to be repugnant to one another, the court will adopt an interpretation that removes the conflict and gives meaning to all terms. In giving full meaning to all the terms of the contract, the courts frequently resort to the circumstances under which the agreement was made, unless the parol evidence rule precludes this approach.

13. The parties perform the contract by doing exactly what they promised to do. As we have seen, it is sometimes difficult to determine exactly what the obligations of the parties are because they are frequently vague in their expression of rights and duties. Through the process of interpretation or construction, however, the courts have been able to work out definite meanings for terms, and this has resulted in some certainty with regard to performance.

The concept of performance should not be confused with that of breach. A party has breached a contract only when his nonperformance is without excuse. Moreover, the courts recognize that in some cases it would be unjust to permit the "victim" to allege and prove a complete breach after substantial performance had been tendered. But for the sake of simplicity, courts usually say that "breach" is nonperformance. Accepting this definition requires one to recognize that the problem of performance also involve a determination of what circumstances excuse it, and what situations require the acceptance of substantial performance plus a money allowance.

Finally, the matter of performance inevitably raises the questions, To whom must performance be tendered? and Who may tender it?

14. Performance is excused when it is legally impossible. In such case, neither party may recover on the contract nor insist on the other's performance. Legal impossibility is different from personal impossibility. Legal impossibility, in effect, means "It cannot be done." Personal impossibility means "I cannot do it." If a person agrees to do a certain act, his inability to do it does not excuse performance. If no one could do it, however, he is excused. Legal impossibility involves one of three situations: (1) death or incapacity of the promisor of a contract that is personal in nature; (2) the supervening of performance; and (3) the destruction of the subject matter essential to performance.

15. It is sometimes said that a party's duty to perform is excused by the nonoccurrence of a condition of the contract. Technically, such a statement is incorrect because no performance is due if a term of the contract suspends it. In that case performance is not excused—it is simply not due. For convenience, however, lawyers tend to regard conditions as part of the law of excuse.

The purpose of inserting a condition in a contract is to postpone the duty of performance or to extinguish that duty under certain circumstances. Thus, a party may provide in the contract that he will not be bound if certain events occur. The events themselves might not provide an excuse for nonperformance, and the condition, therefore, is inserted to protect the party where he otherwise would be unprotected.

Conditions may be created expressly or by implication, and they are said to be "precedent," "concurrent," or "subsequent" in nature.

A fact or event may be a condition because the parties have so stated in the contract. Such a condition is called "express." The intention of the parties that certain events should constitute conditions, however, may be reasonably inferred from their acts and the other terms of the contract. In this case the resulting conditions are said to be "implied."

A precedent condition, either express or implied, arises when the performance of one party is to precede in point of time the performance of the other party. In this case, the party who is to perform first is bound to perform before he can call on the other party to perform. For example, it is implied that when work is to be performed on one side and money is to be paid on the other, the work must be done before payment is made. If the worker does not perform, he may be sued for breach of contract. But the employer cannot be sued for breach merely by nonperformance, unless the worker has tendered his performance. A condition precedent runs in favor of the employer, and he is not liable until the worker first performs. The worker, on the other hand, does not enjoy a condition precedent. Inactivity on his part will result in breach of contract.

A concurrent condition is one that requires the parties to the contract to render performance at the same time. A contract for the sale of goods which mentions no time of payment or delivery is a common example of a situation in which there are concurrent conditions. In this situation, neither the seller nor the buyer needs to perform until performance is tendered by the other.

A condition subsequent is defined by the Restatement of Contracts to be any operative fact that will extinguish a duty to make compensation for breach of contract after the event has occurred.

Conditions subsequent are extremely rare. A common example is a contractual term that suit must be brought within a stated period of time or liability will be discharged. Insurance contracts frequently contain terms that operate to forfeit the insured's rights unless he takes certain action within a prescribed time. These terms are properly said to be conditions subsequent.

16. Under modern law, unless otherwise agreed, all the rights of the parties to a contract may be assigned to third parties except when the assignment would materially change the duty of the other party, increase materially the burden or risk imposed on him by his contract, or impair materially his chance of obtaining return performance.

17. When a party fails to perform his contract, the other party (often known as the "aggrieved party") is entitled to be put in as good a position as he would have enjoyed had the contract been performed. If this principle were literally followed, the only remedy would be one of specific performance, requiring each party to do what he had promised to do. In some civil-law countries, particularly Germany, this principle is literally followed, but in the United States it has been decided that specific performance may not be a very good remedy when the breaching party is reluctant to perform, and the normal remedy is money damages. Indeed, specific performance will be granted only when money damages are shown to be inadequate to put the aggrieved party in as good a position as he would have enjoyed had the contract been performed.

18. Courts divide damages into six different classes: (1) compensatory; (2) consequential or special; (3) punitive or exemplary; (4) incidental; (5) nominal; and (6) liquidated.

"Compensatory" damages are those that place the plaintiff in the economic position he would have enjoyed if the breach had not taken place. But compensatory damages are misnamed because they do not permit the plaintiff to recover for unusual losses not foreseen by the defendant. They may be augmented by consequential or incidental damages in proper cases, but, standing alone, compensatory damages mean only normal damages. Usually, compensatory damages are computed by measuring the difference between the value of the promised performance and the plaintiff's cost to perform.

"Consequential" or "special" damages are those that accrue because of some special or unusual circumstance of the particular contractual relation of the parties. The promisor, in undertaking his commitments, is said to have intended to assume only the risks that normally result from breach of contract. Unless he knows of special circumstances, therefore, he cannot be held liable for consequential damages. But if the promisor has been given notice of facts or should know them from the circumstances and setting of the contract, he may be held liable for consequential damages if these facts or circumstances indicate that a greater loss is probable than normally would flow from a breach. In this case, he is said to have assumed the risk of the unusual loss. Special or consequential damages may consist in loss of employment, loss of business credit, loss of customers, and the like, which result indirectly from breach of contract. They may be recovered in addition to compensatory damages if pleaded and proved to have been foreseeable when the contract was made.

Occasionally, damages in excess of compensation for loss are awarded by way of punishing the defendant. These damages are known as "punitive" or "exemplary" damages. They are seldom awarded in contract cases but find frequent application in the tort law. Breach of promise of marriage is one kind of contract suit in which punitive damages are awarded. In some states, the courts at one time permitted a depositor punitive damages against a bank upon the wrongful dishonor of his checks, but this rule has been changed by the Uniform Commercial Code.

It is said that every breach of contract entitles the aggrieved party to damages. As a corollary of this principle, the aggrieved party is permitted "nominal" damages in those cases in which he has suffered no pecuniary loss or when his loss is too speculative to be recoverable. Nominal damages, as the name implies, is a token amount (like a few cents) given to show the world that the plaintiff was correct in his contentions although unable to show monetary loss. Nominal damages in a sense gives the plaintiff a moral victory.

Frequently the parties to a contract wish to minimize the uncertainties attending the determination of damages, and, accordingly, agree in advance on the amount of damages that will be recoverable in the case of breach. Damages recovered under such as agreement are called liquidated damages. A contract liquidating damages is enforceable if the amount is reasonable, but if it is unreasonable the courts will ignore it and award damages just as if the liquidation clause did not exist.

19. The aggrieved party is bound to do that he reasonably can to keep the amount of his damage as small as possible. This doctrine, known as "the doctrine of avoidable consequence" or the "doctrine of mitigating damages," was not developed to favor defendants, but rather to prevent unnecessary economic waste. To the extent that the aggrieved party fails to mitigate his damages, he is penalized by not being permitted to recover them.

20. Damages must be proved with reasonable certainty. In the absence of such proof, only nominal damages are allowed. This rule is designed to prevent the jury or the judge from speculating as to the amount of damages that should be awarded. Consequently, the rule is sometimes stated that "speculative damages are never allowed." The rule preventing the imposition of speculative damages finds its most frequent application in actions that seek loss of profits for new ventures that have no profit or loss experience.

21. As we have seen, courts in the United States will not grant specific performance if damages are adequate to put the parties in the same economic position they would have enjoyed but for the breach.

The most common application of the remedy of specific performance is found in contracts to sell land. In the eyes of the law, land is unique—like the Watteau painting, no two parcels in the world are alike. Money damages for breach of land contracts are said to be inadequate since they will buy only another piece of land, and not the land that was bargained for. Thus, if one party breaks his contract to sell land, the other can get a decree of specific performance. Specific performance is never decreed to require the performance of personal services, since the United States Constitution has been construed to outlaw slavery and peonage.

8 | Follow-up

If everything in the business world went smoothly or as we would like it to go, there would be no requirement for follow-up. Following up really means trying to make the best of every opportunity to sell your product. These opportunities take various guises and present themselves over a period of time. The various forms of follow-up begin before a proposal is issued and continue well after a transaction has been completed.

TYPES OF FOLLOW-UP

Follow-up falls into several categories: after proposal but before acceptance, after acceptance but before completion, and after completion. In addition, there is the follow-up which takes place before a proposal is ever issued, as an essential part of prospecting for new business.

It is a fact that the more you telephone, visit, or write to a prospect, the more likely you are to do business with that prospect at some time in the future. Therefore, the preproposal follow-up, which consists of continually contacting and recontacting prospects, is of great importance in almost every area of major financial sales. In this sense the term *follow-up* means a continuing succession of telephone calls and visits, all designed to enable the salesman and the prospect to know one another better.

Depending on the number of prospects a salesman has, preproposal follow-up can be very time-consuming. Therefore it is necessary to systematize your efforts to provide a definite, well-defined plan of attack. The deciding factor as to when prospects should be recontacted is the future time at which they might become active buyers of the financial services offered. For instance, if you are attempting to sell financial services to a retail organization such as a department store, it is difficult to get anyone's attention in December and January. September or October and April or May will provide better opportunities. Likewise, if you know that an individual prospect receives an annual bonus in January, the correct time to contact that person is probably some time in December. Certainly midsummer would be inappropriate, since the bonus already received has probably been allocated, and it is too soon to allocate the future one.

Some prospects may become actively interested in your services more than once during the year, and they must be contacted accordingly. Others may be prospects all year long, and continuing close follow-up is necessary in these cases.

In general, the preproposal type of follow-up is one of the more boring tasks a seller of financial services must undertake. It is, however, one that is absolutely essential if the salesman is to obtain a continual flow of proposals and new business.

Once a proposal has been issued, a different type of follow-up is called for. This type is designed to bring the prospect across the line dividing prospect from customer. You must be sure the prospect fully understands the proposal. You also must obtain as much information as you can about the competition.

The objective of this follow-up is to help the prospect decide when the final decision will be made and to determine on what basis it is likely to be made. In most business situations there are interminable delays between the issuance of a proposal and its acceptance or rejection. You must determine why the decision is being delayed, when it will be made, and by whom. If there are changes which would alter the proposal, you must be sure to reissue it and bring it up to date. To accomplish this requires recontacting the prospect by telephone and personal visits and in general continuing to sell as strongly as the situation indicates.

The real selling effort often peaks after the proposal has been issued and the time approaches when a final decision will be made by the prospect. This should be the time of greatest activity on the salesman's part; it is, of course, the time when all of the work he has done with a prospect either succeeds or fails. During this time you should keep asking yourself, "What is it going to take to close this sale?" You must be ready to do whatever is necessary to accomplish that goal.

Some salesmen think this is a time when they can relax, and they often find sales oozing away from them for reasons they may never fully comprehend. If they tried to determine the reasons for these failures, they would probably find that someone else in competition with them had refused to take no for an answer and had continued to sell just as hard as he could. As a result the prospect's mind was changed, in the competitor's favor.

You still cannot relax after the proposal has been issued and accepted. You must continue to follow up as closely as necessary until the sale has been completed.

Once a transaction has been completed and a sale has been made, the routine type of customer contact which is usually considered follow-up comes into play. This type of follow-up has two purposes:

1 To ensure that the purchaser is as satisfied with the transaction as a customer, after the purchase, as he or she was as a prospect, before completion of the sale.
2. To attempt to obtain more business from the same customer.

In most financial sales a great deal of the best business comes from present or former customers. Therefore it is important to let them know that you appreciate their business and you want more of it. This type of follow-up also provides an excellent opportunity to ask for referrals.

TOOLS OF THE TRADE

Salesmen often seem to be completely disorganized, but successful follow-up requires you to be the exception to this rule. In order to organize your follow-up, you need two types of equipment; a virtually unlimited supply of standard 3" × 5" lined index cards, and a large number of letter size manila folders. These and one or two file cabinets constitute the heart of your follow-up system.

You should have an index card for every prospect and present client before contacting anyone, and there should be a manila folder for each person or corporation you have contacted. The folder is used to file copies of all correspondence and sheets of lined paper on which you record the date of every contact and a summary of what was said and done. You need both an index card and a folder for each prospect or client, because they are filed differently.

If you are contacting individuals, your file folders are placed in alphabetical order, so you can put your hand on information concerning a particular person at any time you need to, and the index cards are filed for follow-up according to the following categories:

1. A file of all persons to be contacted in succeeding years; if this is 1981, for example, you should have files for 1982 and 1983 and one for beyond 1983.
2. A file for every month in the present year.
3. A file for the first, second, third, and fourth weeks of the current month.

This plan operates as follows: You contact a prospect or present customer. If this person shows no interest and, in your judgment, should not be followed up on until next year, you would put the card in the next year's follow-up file in alphabetical order. The folder would be returned to your alphabetical file. If you believe the prospect or client should be contacted in June, the folder would still be returned to the alphabetical file, but the index card would be put in your June section. In June you would go through all of the cards for the month and break them down into the first, second, third, and fourth weeks. This system thus gives you a continuing supply of live prospects and existing clients on whom to call.

If you are calling on corporations or businesses, the chances are that they are scattered over a geographical area which may be

Follow-up

fairly wide. In that case your manila folders would be filed according to areas, in alphabetical order. Your index cards would be handled just as if you were soliciting individuals.

The benefits of such a system should be obvious but most salesmen have no effective plan of follow-up. When you start selling you should conduct yourself as if you intend to be a major producer of sales. If you form your work habits accordingly, they will greatly enhance your chances of success. Maintaining a comprehensive, workable follow-up system is an essential part of being completely organized.

The follow-up system suggested above is a simple one which requires a minimum of upkeep. The only thing needed that takes any appreciable time is to match the cards to the folders, and this usually is a matter of mere minutes. It does require persistence, a characteristic that everyone can develop. We can't all be geniuses, but everyone can learn to be persistent.

9 | Negotiating

The term *negotiating* has been defined as "talking about a matter with the idea of coming to terms about it," or "to arrange by means of a discussion of terms." It can also be described as discovering the two sides there are to every question.

Salesmen of financial services, whether to individuals or corporations, often find themselves in a situation where they are negotiating the terms of an agreement of one sort or another. The process usually involves resolving a difference between two parties, but negotiating is not arguing. In a practical sense, it is discussing the terms of an agreement with the idea of enhancing your own position as much as possible.

RULES FOR NEGOTIATING

Over the years I have discovered 16 rules that have been helpful to me during numerous negotiation sessions. They can also be useful to you. However, while the mechanics of negotiating effectively can be learned to some extent, it is an art, not a science.

Only by practice will you become proficient in this skill.

Rule 1 of negotiating is very simple: Be patient. This virtue is particularly effective if the other party in the negotiation lacks patience, because you will find that an impatient person will vacillate and take the path of least resistance, at least as long as you continue to hold to your position. Remember that you have nothing more important to do than closing the present transaction. Be prepared to spend as much time as it takes to settle the matter.

When I expect prolonged meetings which may run through lunch or dinner, I make it a point to bring several diet breakfast bars in my briefcase. I don't mind being patient, but I can't stand being hungry. The psychological impact also may be substantial. When I pull out my breakfast bars, it is obvious that I am prepared for a long siege.

Rule 2 is to find out what the other party's position is in its entirety. It should be obvious that you can't give an answer until you know the question, yet many times negotiations fail because neither party really knows what the other one is attempting to accomplish. Thus neither one makes concessions which would have been not only possible but effective.

I find, as usual, that the direct method is the easiest and most successful. When I need to know what the other party wants, I ask. Further, I continue to ask questions which will clarify the other person's position. This has a peripheral benefit; by asking questions, you appear to be at least somewhat conciliatory. While it may sometimes pay to anger the person with whom you are negotiating, it is usually preferable to at least begin with both parties in a friendly mood. Most people, you will find, would much rather answer questions and describe their position than listen to you make whatever arguments you may have in mind.

After you find out what the other party's position is in its entirety, you must then be sure you know precisely what the other person is trying to accomplish. This is rule 3. Sometimes you will find that this is not clear in the other person's mind. If he doesn't know what he wants, you have no possibility of giving it to him.

I will take a great deal of time to accomplish these first two fundamentals of negotiating, and I find that it is time well spent. The more I induce the other party to talk, the better chance I have of success.

Rule 4 is to find out what your opponent can consider losing and still have the transaction make sense. Rule 5 is to determine what is nonnegotiable, and why. The questioning involved in obtaining the answers to these questions, what can be given up and what is nonnegotiable and why, often helps clarify the other person's position for both parties. Once you have obtained this information, you also are in a position to gauge whether continuing the negotiations can possibly be fruitful. If you can see that there is some unworkable problem, such as the other party wanting to buy something substantially below the market, this is the time to relay the bad news. Sometimes you will find that what was nonnegotiable becomes negotiable when the other party realizes that it is impossible to obtain it.

Rule 6, closely allied to the preceding ones, is to find out what the other party would want if there were no restrictions. This is the time to find out if there are any extras the other party would like to have but considers unobtainable for one reason or another. Some of these extras may actually be easily obtainable as a trade-off for other items which you cannot provide.

Note that five out of the first six rules have to do with clearly demarking the other party's key negotiating positions. The more you know about what this person would ideally like to have, will accept as a bare minimum, and is willing to give up for either or both, the better chance you have to complete the transaction.

Sometime early on in the negotiations, rule 7 applies: Point out what the other party can realistically expect. Probably the other person already knows this, but if not, you can't get the idea across too quickly.

Rules 8–10 have to do with your own position.

Rule 8 is to always ask for more than you logically expect to receive. In some cases, you are going to be negotiating with a person who considers it necessary to get a concession to be satisfied. No matter how little you ask for, such a person must secure a reduction in your terms just to be sure of getting a "good deal." You may also want to give ground in one area to gain in another. Only if you have asked for more than you reasonably expect can you fall back and still receive what you really want. Devious, isn't it? But to negotiate successfully, you must be at least a little devious, if not downright sneaky.

Rule 9 is to avoid revealing your fallback position as long as possible. Here I am directing you to avoid giving the same information you are attempting to derive from the other party, and for precisely the same reasons. Another party who knows of your minimum expectations, will give you just the minimum. The greater the other party feels your minimum expectations are, the more you will receive. This is not the time to be completely candid, although you wish to appear to be doing just that.

Rule 10 is to explain as much as possible why you require what you are asking. This may appear to be contradictory to rule 9, but it is not. It means to build your case as strongly as possible for your maximum expectations. It doesn't mean immediately showing your hand as to the minimum you require.

Rules 11–16 are techniques you can use to help smoothe the process of negotiation.

Rule 11 is: In case of ultimate disagreement, find "the man with the beard." In the first example of successful salesmen given in Chapter 1, an equipment leasing deal was almost lost because a superior of the computer expert who had to accept the transaction had had an unhappy experience with the prospective lessee some time ago. As it happened, this superior was easily distinguishable by his full beard. The salesman salvaged the transaction by directing his prospect's wrath away from himself and onto "the man with the beard."

This transaction made such an impression on me that I have called this redirection of wrath the man-with-the-beard ploy ever since. Over the years I have used the Internal Revenue Service, the Accounting Principles Board, the Federal Reserve Board, the president of the United States, the Department of Defense, and my own top management at various companies as the "man (or men) with the beard." I might say, for example, "I would very much like to accommodate you, Mr. Prospect, but the IRS won't let me," or, "I think your demands are absolutely reasonable, Mr. Prospect, but I know my own management; they are a bunch of damn stick-in-the-muds." Sometimes the individual with whom I am negotiating is going to lose his temper, and I would just as soon he did not lose it at me, because that is the surest way to stop the negotiations. Therefore, whenever I can, I find "the man with the beard."

Rule 12 has something in common with rule 1, since it is merely to keep trying. However, the first rule suggests something of a frame of mind in which you refuse to be excited, whereas this rule calls for a more aggressive posture to be adopted as you continue to try to put the transaction together on the best terms available.

Rule 13 is to know when to stop. You can expect to reach the point in negotiations at which you either have to give in or get out. If you can't do one, you must be ready to do the other. Often the other party will recognize your willingness to walk out on the negotiations and will realize how serious the impasse you have reached is. At that point, you may begin to draw close to an equitable resolution.

Rule 14 is to watch closely for body signs in the other person and avoid showing them yourself, or be prepared to send fake signals. Body signs can reveal anger or impatience, nervousness, or uncertainty. I find that drumming my fingers, for example, will give others the message that I am impatient and speed them along or cause them to make concessions they might not have made had I merely verbalized my position. To utilize this technique fully you have to be at least an amateur actor, but it's all part of the game.

Rule 15 is to keep your temper. When you are angry you are not thinking, and in negotiating you must think constantly. Further, once you lose your temper, the chances are that all negotiating will end. Thus you may win the battle but lose the war.

When the negotiations are drawing to a close, it is time to practice rule 16: Be realistic in your expectations. While rule 8 directs you to ask for more than you expect to receive, there are limits to what you can expect. It is as foolish to expect to be paid more than goods and services are worth as it is to expect to pay less for them than they are worth.

I have not suggested that you should attempt "intimidation" in negotiations, a tactic suggested by some well-known authors on the subject. Most knowledgeable individuals would either be offended or laugh at such an attempt. Remember, you want to continue to do business with those you are negotiating with. To humiliate, intimidate, or offend them would be a serious mistake.

10 | Closing

The first nine chapters of this book have shown you how to prepare yourself psychologically, mentally, and physically to face the hard, cruel world of obstinate prospects. You have been shown how to prospect, interview, issue proposals, follow up, and negotiate. But you still have not been shown how to make a sale, and that, after all, is the object of this book—to improve your chances for success as a salesman of big-ticket financial services.

In working with salesmen I have found that many of them do quite well at all the preliminaries that have been described, but they still lack the intestinal fortitude (a euphemism for what we used to call *guts*) to corner a prospect and not only ask for the sale but insist upon it. This process is called *closing*. The whole secret of closing is to keep asking for the business until you get it. The accompanying checklist for closing sales lists the procedures to be used in doing this, and the examples which follow illustrate how the procedures can be applied.

An important factor in closing a sale is the psychology of the prospects to whom you are trying to sell goods or services. They

> ### CHECKLIST FOR CLOSING SALES
>
> 1. List the advantages of your product or services and make sure that your prospect understands them.
> 2. List the possible disadvantages of the alternative to your proposal, that is, another proposal or a delay, and discredit these alternatives as much as possible. Make sure that your prospect agrees.
> 3. Ask for the sale. Assume that you will obtain the sale and keep asking until you do.
> 4. If refused, find out why. Resell the advantages, point out the disadvantages again, and again ask for the sale. Assume that you will get it.
> 5. When your prospect's objections don't make sense, there is some hidden objection that he has not yet revealed to you. This you must find out if you are to close the sale. Don't be bashful about asking, and keep asking until you find out what the problem may be.
> 6. Answer objections patiently and cheerfully. Remember, your objective is to make your prospects feel that you like them, that you value their friendship, and that their welfare is one of your main considerations.
> 7. Don't be hesitant to show appreciation and let prospects know that you value their business.

probably are interested in obtaining the benefits of what you are selling, or you would not have gotten to this point. At the same time, they have a human fear of making a mistake. It stands to reason, therefore, that in closing you should stress the positive, that is, the advantages of the goods or services offered, and do your best to allay the hidden fears that are behind most lost sales.

EXAMPLES OF CLOSINGS: FAINT HEART NEVER WINS

Suppose you are selling securities to a wealthy, retired individual. The prospects are that this person's main concern, aside from making money, is not losing money. Your approach might be something like this:

Closing

> Mr. Prospect, our firm has examined these securities with extreme care. Our primary purpose is to produce income for you. But we also want to be able to assure you, as much as humanly possible, that this investment will not only make money for you now but will continue to grow with maximum safety.
>
> It is true that there are other investments which could be more productive. Unfortunately, such investments carry a much greater additional risk. Therefore we felt that these investments were not for you. The securities we have suggested have minimum downside risk, as well as substantial room for capital appreciation over the longer term. That's why we think they are for you.
>
> Incidentally, you are extremely fortunate because the timing on acquiring these securities is excellent—they are now selling at the lower part of their historical price range. With your permission, I will get these orders in immediately, and we will have your portfolio in apple pie order by the end of the week. What is your social security number? I need it to open the account.

What are you doing in this conversation?

1. You try to build confidence in the product.
2. You point out the dangers inherent in an alternative strategy.
3. You indicate that you and your firm are both very much interested in the client's welfare.
4. You indicate that the time to act is *now!*
5. You start to obtain the information needed to help the prospect overcome inertia and get moving, so you can actually open the account.

Sometimes this is called an *assumptive close*, in which you assume that the prospect will buy your goods or services, and you proceed until you are stopped. This is the tactic the life insurance agent uses in placing the pen in your hand while placing the application before you, only it is on a somewhat more sophisticated basis. Strangely enough, it works. It works, I believe, because most people who take the time to talk about buying something over a long period really do want to buy it, and all they need is a gentle nudge to get them moving.

Suppose the prospect in this case says, "No, Mr. Salesman, I think I want to wait and think this over." What should you say then? Perhaps something like this:

Mr. Prospect, I know that you want to be very, very careful with this investment. Believe me, my firm and I are even more interested in being careful with your investment, since we hope to get referral business from you. It is to our best interests if an important man in the community such as yourself is completely satisfied.

At the same time, you and I both know that it is not only what you buy but at what price you buy it that influences the success of your investment program. Now it is true that these securities may go somewhat lower over the course of time before they go higher. At this point, however, it appears more reasonable to assume that they are going to increase in price before they decrease. In any event, since they are near the bottom of their trading ranges over the past few years, it would appear that, based on general accepted criteria, they are quite cheap at these prices.

Let me tell you what I am afraid of—once you have seen these low prices, if the price should go up a little bit, your natural inclination will be to wait until they come down again, and that may never happen. Personally, I hate to chase securities, and I find that many people make this mistake. They don't buy at 100; at 105 they are willing to pay 101; the security's price retreats to 103; they miss their opportunity; now it moves to 107, which, after all, is only a 7 percent increase, but then they want to buy at 105, which they never have the opportunity to do. They could, of course, have bought all they wanted at 100. Often, they buy at an inflated price, which then retreats.

In any event, we are suggesting that you phase in your purchases over a period of time, so let's start *now*. If we start *now* and prices do turn downward, we will have the opportunity to take advantage of it. And if they go up, we will have purchased at least part of your portfolio at today's prices. Now, what is your social security number?

Here you try to reinforce the original argument, making the most of the best selling feature of the program, minimizing the risk, and attempting to instill fear of loss through failure to act. You also try to bring in some subtle flattery and to convince the prospect that both you and your firm are truly interested in his well-being, if only from a self-serving standpoint.

Now suppose the prospect still refuses to move ahead. What do you do now? The answer should be obvious. You try again:

> Mr. Prospect, I can sympathize with your doubts. But we have been discussing this matter and going up the learning curve together for the past few months. I think we both have a fairly good idea of what you want to accomplish. Both my company and I believe these securities will accomplish your investment goal.
>
> Evidently we have missed something. Is there some problem with this portfolio that we are not aware of? Or is there something in your personal situation that we have not grasped? I think we both agree that these securities are priced "right," so now would seem the time to move ahead. Yet obviously, something is troubling you. What is it?

For the third time, you are going over the plusses, downplaying the negatives, and asking for action. At this point, it should be clear that you don't have the entire picture. Therefore you attempt to find the hidden objection, or the cause of the delay. You might find a number of things are responsible. The prospect doesn't have the funds available; he has been talking with someone else and has promised not to take action until he has talked with them again; or he has read or heard something that has caused him to question the wisdom of this move. What you must do is find out precisely what is holding up the party, and the best way to do this is through direct questioning.

If he doesn't have the funds now, you must find out when he will have them and try to arrange a purchase schedule to make the most of his availability of funds. If he has talked to someone else, you must try to find out who and why and what that party is suggesting. If he has been talking with the salesman for a competitor, the best procedure would be to find out precisely what the competitor is recommending and why. You might say something like this:

> Mr. Prospect, I can well understand your wanting to get another opinion on a matter of this importance. However, after examining the recommendations our competitor has made, I find that they are not really substantially different from what we have been recommending. Therefore, I have to agree with them. On the other hand, I think our analysis has been more thorough and personalized, and therefore we really deserve your business. I am sure that as a businessman you attempt to do business with those who give you the greatest service, so I feel that you will want to do business with us. So let's get started.

If the competitor has come up with an entirely different proposal, you might say something like this:

> Mr. Prospect, I know the competitor that you have mentioned, and they do an excellent job. However, I think you will find that in this case their proposal is geared for the average investor, as opposed to a special case such as yours. This proposal of theirs appears to me to be the standard, common, off-the-shelf-type portfolio that they pump out to the mass market. It is completely suitable for the average investor, but it doesn't lend itself to your particular needs. Let me be specific.

At this point, you should point out the disadvantages, as you perceive them, in the competitor's program. You would not denigrate the competitor in any way but would merely point out that its proposal was not appropriate because it had not spent the time developing the personal relationship that you had. Again, you would ask for the business.

The long and the short of this whole closing process is to keep closing until there is nowhere to go, that is, until you are convinced that the prospect is not going to move at that point. In most cases of personal sales, I won't give up until I have closed at least one-half dozen times, and sometimes even more.

Sometimes it is very difficult to retain your patience and sense of humor during this process, but this is a must. I suggest that you try to get across to your prospects that you like them, that their best interests are what you have at heart, and that no matter how many times you have to close, you are not losing your patience or becoming irritated with them. Sometimes I have even gone so far as to tell them that they might as well give in now, because I am going to keep after them until they do. And sometimes that is precisely what is needed to close a sale.

At other times, the closing happens almost naturally. Some years ago I worked for a major stock brokerage firm in the downtown office. After a year or so, I left this firm to go with a smaller one in the suburbs. One day, while reading the broad tape (the digest of news information from Dow Jones), I noticed a rather bedraggled individual come in wearing sandals and a sports shirt outside bleached khaki trousers. Since he was only 5 feet, 3 inches tall, his appearance was not too prepossessing. From my previous experience I recognized him as one of the largest traders in the city, however. I greeted him by name, which seemed to surprise him, and offered to give him any assistance I could. I helped make him comfortable in the office, and over the next month or so I made myself as useful as possible to him.

After about four or five weeks, during which time he had been using my telephone to call orders downtown to his main account, I said, "Sam, don't you think it is time we opened an account for you out here? It would be a lot more convenient. What's your social security number?" This was the beginning of a long and profitable relationship because he eventually transferred his entire account to our firm.

Note that prior to the closing I had done virtually nothing that could be called selling. All I did was try to make him as comfortable as possible and, at the same time, indicate that I recognized his importance. As it happened, he had originally wandered into our office because he had had an argument with the firm with whom he had been dealing. Strangely enough, his principal complaint was that they did not give him enough service. Over the next year or so, I picked him up every morning at his home, drove him to the office, bought him breakfast, and sat side by side with him during the entire working day. During that time I had a direct line put in which connected directly to our floor trader at the New York Stock Exchange. At the end of the day, we would go over the day's activities, have a cup of coffee, and I would take him home. Not only did I benefit from his business, which took quite a toll in nervous energy, but when it became known that he was working through me, other traders became my clients merely because they were following his activity.

An interesting question—and one I have never been able to fully answer in my own mind—is why someone who would have been greeted with open arms in any brokerage office in the city, and particularly by brokers with much more experience than I had at the time, chose to do business with me. If I had to come up with one reason, I think it was because I made it easy for him to buy.

In selling to a corporation, the closing process is somewhat different than it is in closing with an individual. You usually will have issued a detailed, written proposal to the company, and an integral part of the closing mechanism is to go over the proposal paragraph by paragraph to make sure that the prospect understands every facet of the proposed agreement. Once that has been accomplished, closing with a corporation is no different from closing with an individual. It comes down to asking for the business and continuing to ask until you are certain that you have it or can't get it.

Many times a corporate sale closing is complicated by the fact that your contact must obtain approval from others. Nevertheless, it is important to close so far as the individual is concerned. You could say: "Mr. Prospect, if I understand you correctly, you are in favor of our proposition. You must clear this with your Board of Directors, but, as far as you are concerned, you are 100 percent for it. Am I correct?" Statements of this type are necessary to be sure that when others who are involved examine the proposition, it will receive the full support of your contact. If this person has any doubts, the closing is the time to discover them and answer any objections, hidden or otherwise.

Sometimes the assumptive close is the ideal way to close a corporate sale. Some years ago I was calling on a major cement company. Over a long period, we had discussed in detail the advantages of leasing their vehicles. He had agreed that it seemed like the right thing to do, but when I had asked him if he wanted to give me the go ahead immediately, he had demurred.

I arranged to visit him again at his office, and again I went over all the advantages of our proposal. But this time I began to fill out the form which was necessary to initiate the transaction, asking various questions about the corporation, and so on. Finally, I asked him to sign the application, and he did. At no time had he explicitly agreed to go forward with this transaction; I merely assumed that he would do so. Once I began to prepare to complete the transaction, he went along with it as if he had been planning to do so from the beginning. This particular sale taught me a lesson: Individuals act as individuals, even when they are working for corporations. Sometimes, even though they want to buy, they need that last little nudge to get them over the edge.

11 | Getting home office support

It may or may not be true that behind every successful man stands a woman. However, it is absolutely certain that behind every successful salesperson there stands at least one and sometimes many supporting workers. These people don't earn large commission checks and don't get to travel or eat in expensive restaurants, and their positions provide very little glamour or excitement. But without them, the best salesperson in the world will fail.

As a salesman of big-ticket financial services, you will be only as good as the support you receive, and your success will be directly related to that support. You will regularly require secretarial assistance and various technical services, depending on the nature of your business. Without them, you will be virtually helpless. There also will be times when you require special services, and the way to be sure to get them is to prepare well in advance. Your attitude toward those supporting you will directly affect their attitude toward you and their performance for you.

Salesmen often forget that their co-workers are not enjoying the same benefits they do and do not have the same incentive to complete transactions. The way to arouse their interest and provide that incentive is to give them reason to have good feelings about you. Some things you can do to inspire these feelings are listed in the accompanying checklist.

CHECKLIST FOR MAINTAINING GOOD RELATIONS WITH CO-WORKERS

1. Make sure you know as much as possible about every technical or office operation that can affect the success of your sales effort.
2. Make sure you know as much as possible about all the paperwork involved in supporting your sales efforts.
3. Indicate a genuine interest in co-workers as people and the work they do.
4. Whenever possible, show appreciation to co-workers.

My first experience in big-ticket financial sales was with a large brokerage house. I had only been there a short time when I noticed that their most successful salesman was generally in the office quite early, often before most of the other salesmen. Despite the fact that he was very busy, he seemed to make it a point to say hello or good morning to everyone working in what we called the cage, or back office. Every month or so, he brought the women working there a box of candy or some other delicacy, and he went out of his way to chat with the young man in charge.

Considering this was an individual who was stingy with his time even with wealthy clients, this puzzled me. I finally asked him why he took so much time with relatively unimportant people. His answer was that far from being relatively unimportant, these people were most definitely relatively important. He advised me that one of the best ways to be a success in any business is to know precisely what your co-workers are doing and why they are doing it. This is the best way to be assured that you understand their problems and that you will be able to avoid difficulties in completing and processing your sales. Further, since their attitude toward you is affected by your attitude toward them, the friendlier you are to them, the friendlier they are to you, and the harder they will work when you need special services. I greatly respected this individual, and I resolved to remember his advice.

Later, when I was able to obtain a major trader as a client, I made it a point to travel to our home office in New York to meet the head of our floor traders. I was able to cajole him into installing a direct line from my desk to the floor of the New York Stock Exchange. I also made it a point to meet all of the individuals who had anything to do with my customer's trading and get to know them on a first-name basis.

This customer was difficult to deal with, since he was constantly attempting to obtain special privileges which the New York Stock Exchange would not allow us to give him. I had to be very careful or I would find both myself and my firm in violation of stock exchange regulations. To avoid this, I often needed service above and beyond the norm. So I visited my supporting co-workers in New York at least once every few weeks. Sometimes I was able to have a drink with someone after work, but often I spent most of my time there merely expressing my appreciation. Without their complete cooperation I would never have been able to service that customer and I would have lost a great deal of commission business.

When I began in the equipment leasing business, I made it a point to understand every form we used and every procedure we followed. This enabled me to avoid making problems for those in the home office. It also allowed the workers to process my transactions much more rapidly than those of other salesmen who had been working for the company for many years.

The ultimate in poor co-worker relations was practiced by a salesman who worked for me. He constantly griped about everything, he magnified every error, and he seldom had a good word for anyone. Perhaps by coincidence (but probably not), the office work done for him continued to deteriorate and was noticeably poorer than that done for every other salesman. After this situation had been brought to his attention rather forcibly many times, I could see a gradual change in his attitude. With that change, he began to get much better office support.

12 | A note to the saleswoman

It has been brought to my attention that there is a glaring omission in this book. I have not considered women as executive salespersons of financial services. The omission was not conscious; the fact is that few women have held these positions in the past. When I began the book in 1979, my company, for example, had never had a woman salesperson. Since that time (quite recently, as a matter of fact), we have promoted one of our women employees to a position where she travels as a sales representative covering a number of distant states. Other women have taken positions as stockbrokers and investment counselors.

In this chapter, therefore, I will review the book with an eye to the particular problems women face as salespersons, as I perceive them.

Chapter 1, "The Making of a Big-Ticket Financial Salesman," might just as easily read "The Making of a Big-Ticket Financial Salesperson." Everything in it is as true for a woman as it is for a man. The beginning of this chapter, in fact, recognizes that the field is open to women.

In Chapter 2, "Projecting the Image of Success," the first section, "How to Get Your Story Across," applies precisely the same to women as it does to men. In the second section, "How to Look the Part," of course, the woman's situation is much different. The problem women face in this respect is to remain feminine but appear businesslike, as Chapter 2 notes. It is a mistake to try to look like a man, but if a woman's clothes accentuate her physical attributes, she is asking for trouble. The successful businesswomen I have met dress conservatively, yet in a feminine manner which does not try to obscure the fact that they are women.

The next six chapters on preliminary procedures apply to women just as they do to men. This includes Chapter 3, "Selling Is a State of Mind"; 4, "What to Do Before the First Interview"; 5, "Prospecting"; 6, "The Interview"; 7, "Issuing Proposals"; and 8, "Follow-up."

Chapter 9, "Negotiating," calls for some additional thoughts, however. I have found that women in business often fall into the habit of attempting to appear "tough," and in my view, this is a mistake. Men generally are antagonistic to other men who try to project such an image, and in women, it seems almost certain to arouse negative reactions. Furthermore, unless the woman is quite exceptional, it can make her appear ludicrous. A woman who attemps to be unbelievably tough subjects herself to the same ridicule as a man who appears effeminate.

Men are likely to underestimate a woman's business skills, and in negotiating this can be a considerable advantage for the woman. But, even more than a man, a woman has to be careful never to lose her temper or to show a great deal of emotion. Many men will be only too eager to attribute any sign of temperament in a saleswoman to her femininity. On balance, a woman probably has an advantage in negotiating, provided she is as well informed as a man would be and controls her emotions

Chapters 10, "Closing," and 11, "Getting Home Office Support," are, of course, precisely the same for women as they are for men. The summary which follows, "Selling Can Be Fun, or Winning Beats Losing," is probably more true for a woman who has had to fight to obtain and hold her position than it is for a man who hasn't had to overcome the same barriers.

In the future I may write a book devoted solely to the opportunities available to women in selling and to the problems they encounter. If women would write me in care of the publisher with their comments or stories of their experiences, I would greatly appreciate it.

Summary:
Selling can be fun, or winning beats losing

This book was written to help you determine if you are temperamentally suited to be a salesman of big-ticket financial services. It has discussed in detail the preparation necessary to become successful in this field and pointed out the pitfalls of such activities. You have been supplied with both theoretical and practical advice on how to be successful in selling these services. The book has covered everything from the salesman's state of mind and appearance to the finer points of interviewing, prospecting, negotiating, and closing sales. Both new and experienced salesmen have been given encouragement and advice on how to be successful on a continuing basis.

Throughout this book, a number of challenges which you will face as a salesman have been examined. Meeting most of these challenges will require great concentration and dedication on your part. But, there is more to selling big-ticket financial services than just a great deal of hard work. It provides a tremendous amount of satisfaction and a pay scale that is probably the highest in the world.

On the average, people working in government, business, or industry have very little opportunity to stretch their performance to the limits of their ability. In many positions, they are not encouraged to show initiative or to use their intelligence. On the contrary, they are often forced to become virtual robots. Big-ticket financial sales is one of the few areas remaining where employees have the satisfaction of achieving success through their own efforts, and where financial rewards are almost always in direct proportion to an individual's successes.

So you ought to enjoy selling! Successful big-ticket selling can give you both pride of accomplishment and the thrill of high-stakes gambling. Many salesmen, as a matter of fact, seem to fluctuate between depression and euphoria as their efforts meet with comparatively more or less success.

If you can summon the energy, will, and dedication needed to follow the techniques outlined and follow them faithfully, you will not only be a successful salesman but, what is more important, a successful person. As you improve your physical and mental condition, you will be earning your living in the manner you have chosen and realizing the psychological satisfaction of performing a difficult task with grace and flair.

Yes, winning does beat losing, and selling can really be fun!